Autumn
at the Farmers
Market

GAIL GRECO'S
LITTLE
Bed & Breakfast
COOKBOOK SERIES

Autumn at the Farmers Market

Text by GAIL GRECO

Photographs by TOM BAGLEY

RUTLEDGE HILL PRESS
Nashville, Tennessee

Published in Nashville, Tennessee, by Rutledge Hill Press, Inc., 211 Seventh Avenue North, Nashville, Tennessee 37219. Distributed in Canada by H.B. Fenn & Company, Ltd., 34 Nixon Road, Bolton, Ontario L7E 1W2. Distributed in Australia by Millennium Books, 33 Maddox Street, Alexandria NSW 2015. Distributed in New Zealand by Tandem Press, 2 Rugby Road, Birkenhead, Auckland 10. Distributed in the United Kingdom by Verulam Publishing, Ltd., 152a Park Street Lane, Park Street, St. Albans, Hertfordshire AL2 2AU.

Photographs by Tom Bagley
Photo art direction and styling by Gail Greco
Food styling assistance by Priscilla Powers, Dennis Hayden, Michael Carnahan, and Lue Crane
Editorial assistance by Tricia Conaty
Fall prop assistance by Homeplace Everlastings in Hagerstown, Maryland
Cover and book design by Gore Studio, Inc.
Text layout and typesetting by John Wilson Design
All recipes selected and edited for the home kitchen by Gail Greco
Photo on page 96 by Gerald Liebert

ON THE FRONT COVER: GOOD EARTH PRODUCE IN OLNEY, MARYLAND
PHOTO OPPOSITE TITLE PAGE: PUMPKIN PUDDING FROM INN AT CEDAR FALLS, RECIPE ON PAGE 98.

Greco, Gail.
    Autumn at the farmers market / Gail Greco ; photography by Tom Bagley.
        p. cm.
    Includes index.
    ISBN 1-55853-435-9
    1. Cookery, American. 2. Bed and breakfast accommodations—United States—Directories. I. Title.
    TX715.G811467   1996
    641.5973—dc20   96-30492
                                                  CIP

Printed in the United States of America

1 2 3 4 5 6 7 8 9 — 00 99 98 97 96

The crisp fall air beckons
me to light the hearth
fires. I employ the wooden
bellows he made with his
creative hands, wishing
I could return its
life-giving breath to his
own hearth so that it
might blaze again
near mine.

Contents

Other Books in This Series

❧

The Test Kitchen for the
Cooking Association of Country Inns

Although all inn recipes are tried-and-true and served at the inns all the time, the recipes in this cookbook have been further verified and tested for accuracy and clarification for the home kitchen.

The cooking seal of approval that accompanies this book, means that every recipe has been tested in inn kitchens other than the source, and that the association test kitchen has been satisfied that the recipe is proven and worthy of preparing.

The test kitchen is under the leadership of association founder Gail Greco, with Charla Honea and other editors at Rutledge Hill Press assisting. The prestigious list of kitchen testers includes:

～o～

DAVID CAMPICHE, *Chef/Owner*
The Shelburne Inn • Seaview, Washington

YVONNE MARTIN, *Chef/Owner*
The White Oak Inn • Danville, Ohio

DEBBIE MOSSIMAN, *Chef/Owner*
Swiss Woods • Lititz, Pennsylvania

PATRICK RUNKEL, *Chef/Owner*
October Country Inn • Bridgewater Corners, Vermont

CLAUDIA RYAN, *Chef/Owner*
Windflower Country Inn • Great Barrington, Massachusetts

LAURA SIMOES, *Chef/Owner*
The Inn at Maplewood Farm • Hillsborough, New Hampshire

ELIZABETH TURNEY, *Chef/Owner*
Bear Creek Lodge • Victor, Montana

MARION YADON, *Chef/Owner*
Canyon Villa Bed & Breakfast • Sedona, Arizona

Sweet Potato Waffles, recipe on page 13

A Day in the Country
Offers a Plentiful Crop and Much More

It was a crisp sunny day. With its change of leaves and its culinary bounty, the day brought a new and fulfilling future. My traveling partner and I had taken a ride to the mountains, about two hours from home—in search of colorful leaves to collect, antiques shops to browse, old barns and country churches to photograph, an apple-cider mill to refill our empty jugs, and most importantly, foods from fresh fields to purchase at rickety wooden roadside stands.

Our treasure trove of fall finds eclipsed our senses. We were caught up in the fever of the season and all its alluring temptations. Suddenly it was too late to drive home. We needed a place to stay—a motel, of course. There wasn't much else to choose in 1981. At least we didn't think so, until we finally happened upon an attractive old farmhouse with a curious sign: Fine Food and Lodging. "Must mean this family's home does the advertising for a motel and restaurant somewhere nearby," I suggested. Little did I know that a knock at the front door of the farmhouse would not only usher me inside but also unleash a whole new world.

It was the world of bed-and-breakfast/country inns—lodging alternatives that only those who meandered about back roads would find. In those days, there were few such abodes and even fewer guidebooks to tell you about them. An enchanting night of dinner by candlelight in an intimate dining room, rapturous robes for the trip to a shared bathroom down the hall, and a bedcovering of feather comforters at the farmhouse with four guest rooms—all left me with the notion that things would never be the same again. This autumn's bounty would prove to offer much more than a bushel of Rome Beauties or a basket of

crookneck squash. I had stayed at my first country inn—the former home of a farmer. The rest is history. Autumn had cast its spell that year in a most promising way. But—literally and lyrically—fall has a habit of bringing about such seeds of change.

These days, with the emphasis on fresh, healthier food, the farmers market is often the catalyst , the reason to go for a drive in search of the nearest market. As kids, my brothers, sister, and I would hop into the station wagon as our family headed out from the city for a drive in search of brown bags full of sweet potatoes, red peppers, apples, berries, and homemade breads. Sometimes it meant going to a specialized farm just for one item, such as the onion farm for Vidalias, Dad's favorite, or bunches of earthy beets and spinach, the things Mom kept an eye out for, always canvassing the vegetable bins. Each time we returned home, we were all inspired. . . Dad more so than anyone else. One day he came home from the country and ended up sketching out plans for a backyard shed in the shape of an overgrown orange pumpkin! The shed never materialized but he talked about building that pumpkin—season after season—for a couple of decades. In the meantime, he settled for another fantasy, something much larger than a shed: a house—in the shape of the dairy barns we encountered when shopping in the country.

Autumn at the farmers market can do that to you. There is something memorable, comforting, almost primordial about shopping for the earth's gifts and passing some time with the folks who planted them—whether you find this bounty in the country or in the city at a greenstand. Shopping at open-air markets is a way of life in Europe where farm markets reign supreme over supermarkets. I have visited many in Europe and one stands out in Oporto, Portugal. Farmers sell everything here. An elderly widow offers a whole booth full of nothing but garlic bulbs, a poultry farmer sells live chickens from portable coops, and ladies shred cabbage at large steel wheels for those who want to go home and cook the country's famous native soup, *caldo verde* (green soup). Visiting the markets gives you a greater appreciation of the plight of the farmer, while offering direct support to the small farmers. We don't ever want to lose them.

I have also visited markets across the United States and love going to farm markets in any season, but the fall holds some sort of magic for me. Each farmer has something different to offer. You cannot help but snatch up a few small white eggplants or perennial favorites, such as homemade preserves, spiced butters, whimsical winter and late-summer squashes, farm cheeses like goat cheese, corn and other salsas, and bouquets of flowers. (I always buy late-blooming sunflowers just to ensure that I see a smile from the passenger's seat, brimming over at me all the way home.)

The farmers' dedicated months of tilling, toiling, and nurturing everything from red peppers to butter lettuces and ornamental cabbages set the stage for irresistible just-picked buys. Whether sold at the larger weekly markets or at roadside stands, the farmers' yields make you yearn to rush home, cook, and eat.

After I spend an autumn day motoring from market to market, my pantry at home takes on the look of a well-stocked old-fashioned general store. I get anxious to begin preparing slow-simmering suppers with stockpots of veggies and broths, while I sip a varietal wine just brought home from a postharvest country vineyard and winery. We crank up the wood-burning fireplace, break crusty breads, and munch on them with cheeses just purchased from a farmhouse kitchen, and begin peeling the apples for a salad or cobbler.

The farmers market is my inspiration for planning fall meals, and it is much the same for chefs and cooks at small inns nationwide. Chef François de Melogue, of the Old Drover's Inn in Dover Plains, New York, took me with him to a tomato farm where we twisted robust, red tomatoes from their gnarly vines. Later, he showed me the secrets of his spaghetti sauce. The fresh sauce was heavenly. In fall, such ruby gems are only available if you buy the vine-ripened tomatoes—much more expensive but well worth the price.

At Stonehedge, a country inn in Tyngsboro, Massachusetts, Chef David Blessing took me through a cornfield where I became a believer in the idea that the corn does whisper before it's born, or was it just the leaves rustling in the breeze like taffeta? Back at the inn, we had a New England clambake—lobster, clams, and the corn cooked in seaweed in a giant cauldron. The sweet corn, and nearly as sweet seafood, left my taste buds in mourning after I left the inn.

Country inn cooking is regional fare that is determined by what is made and grown at local farms. Some inns have their own rows of produce in bloom, determining the autumn menu. And there are farm bed-and-breakfasts that may even have a rooster and some hens on the loose, providing fresh eggs for the morning. Autumn and bed-and-breakfast inns go together. A day in the country during this time of year is even more satisfying when it includes an overnight stay at a quaint B&B.

When you are harvest bound, who knows where the road may take you—somewhere certainly as rich and fulfilling for you as my journey to that first inn so long ago while in search of autumn at the farmers market.

The Dairy Barn

Rum Raisin Cheddar Spread

‿∾‿

I have enjoyed sitting in the grand Queen Victoria B&B for teatime where I have sampled this delightful spread with fruit and crackers. Farm markets are filled with homemade spreads. Meantime try this one, using some farm-market cheese. You will need to start this several hours ahead of serving time.

SIGNS OF THE SEASON AT HOMEPLACE

1	cup plump organic raisins
1/3	cup dark rum
6	ounces cream cheese, softened
8	ounces sharp cheddar cheese, shredded

MAKES 1 1/2 CUPS

Soak the raisins in the rum for 1 hour. Whirl the cream cheese and cheddar cheese until smooth. Add the raisins with the rum and process briefly, enough to chop the raisins coarsely. Chill for a few hours before serving with crackers or vegetables.

—THE QUEEN VICTORIA

Apple Lasagne

～～

The traditional eggs-and-cheese pasta dish is served here as a breakfast dish or as a fruit course. The inn's recipe calls for making two pans of lasagne. You may make this ahead and freeze but defrost thoroughly before baking. The inn serves the lasagne with a sauce of $2/3$ cup of non-dairy hazelnut cream mixed with $1/3$ cup of sour cream. A crème anglaise also makes a nice sauce, or mix sugar and water with an almond extract.

Filling		Topping	
16	lasagne noodles (about 1 pound)	6	tablespoons (³/₄ stick) butter
3	pounds ricotta cheese	³/₄	cup all-purpose flour
4	eggs	1	teaspoon cinnamon
3	16-ounce cans apple-pie filling	¹/₂	cup rolled quick oats
2	teaspoons vanilla extract	³/₄	cup firmly packed brown sugar
		¹/₂	cup finely chopped nuts of choice

MAKES 16 SERVINGS

APPLE BLOSSOM OF SPRING GIVES WAY TO FRUIT IN FALL.

In a large pot of boiling, salted water cook lasagne noodles until al dente. Drain and rinse under cold water. Return to the pot with a small amount of cold water to cover the noodles.

Preheat the oven to 350°. In a large bowl combine the ricotta cheese, eggs, pie filling, and vanilla. Set aside.

Coat the bottom and sides of 2 9x13-inch baking pans with cooking oil spray. Layer 4 noodles across the bottom of each pan, overlapping slightly. Spread half of the filling over the noodles. Cover with another layer of noodles. Evenly divide the remaining apple-pie filling over the noodles. Set aside.

Prepare the topping. In a medium bowl, use your hands to mix together all ingredients until coarse crumbs form. Spread evenly over the apples in each pan. Bake 45 minutes or until topping is golden brown and filling is bubbly. Remove from the oven and let lasagne set 15 to 20 minutes before serving with the sauce.

— THE LAKEHOUSE ON GOLDEN POND

[5]

Early Fall Finds at the Farmers Market

Corn and Swiss Cheese Flan

⤳o⤳

Easy and heartwarming, this side dish may be served over blanched zucchini and carrots cut julienne. It is even pleasant as a brunch dish aside eggs and ham. The green chile is optional. What a view of Puget Sound a guest gets while eating this flan from high on a bluff overlooking a charming Washington city.

2	cups fresh (or frozen) corn kernels		1	cup grated Swiss cheese
2	extra large eggs, lightly beaten		1	large green chile, finely chopped
1	teaspoon sugar		2	teaspoons chopped fresh or dried chives
1½	tablespoons sour cream			Salt and pepper to taste
1	cup scalded milk			
⅓	cup plus 1 tablespoon biscuit mix			

MAKES 6 SERVINGS

Preheat the oven to 350°. Place the corn in a food processor and process (about 20 seconds). Add all of the other ingredients and process until smooth (about 45 seconds). Grease 6 (3-inch) ramekins, filling each evenly with the flan mixture. Place ramekins on a baking sheet. Bake the flan for 20 to 30 minutes or until set. Slip out onto individual plates and serve.

— RAVENSCROFT INN

Oatmeal Apple Cider and Raspberry Pancakes with Cinnamon Cream

꒰ఞ꒱

Fresh-cooking oatmeal pancakes with the smell of all that cinnamon in the batter put you in a fall kind of mood right from the start! Seven Sisters does that to you as soon as you walk through its marvelous Victorian front door.

Pancakes		Topping	
2	cups biscuit mix	1/2	pint whipping cream
1	cup quick cooking oats	2	tablespoons sugar
2	tablespoons cinnamon	1	teaspoon vanilla extract
2	eggs	2	tablespoons sour cream
1 to 2	cups apple cider	1	tablespoon cinnamon
1	13-ounce package frozen raspberries	1	pint fresh raspberries, for garnish

MAKES 4 SERVINGS

In a large bowl combine the pancake mix, oats, and cinnamon. Beat the eggs in a small dish and blend into the dry mixture. Stir in the apple cider slowly, adding more for thinner pancakes. Set aside.

Place the frozen raspberries in a plastic bag and crush with a mallet. Stir the crushed berry bits into the batter.

Lightly oil a hot griddle. Spoon the batter onto the griddle, in 3-inch diameter circles. Cook until golden brown on each side.

Prepare topping by beating together the cream and sugar until dissolved. Blend in the vanilla, sour cream, and cinnamon. Mix well, adding more sour cream for desired thickness. Serve with the pancakes and top with raspberries.

—SEVEN SISTERS INN

Cinnamon and Fresh Corn Griddle Cakes with Cranberry Butter

Pancakes made with corn and cornmeal take on a buttery flavor. These are irresistible and outrageous with the cranberry butter, which also tastes great on tea scones. Make the butter a few hours or even a few days ahead of time. Serve with a maple or other syrup, if desired.

Cranberry Butter

- 1 cup fresh or frozen cranberries (or dried cranberries soaked in boiling water for 5 minutes)
- 1¼ cups sugar
- ½ cup (1 stick) unsalted butter
- ¼ cup Grand Marnier

Pancakes

- 1¾ cups all-purpose flour
- ½ cup finely milled yellow cornmeal
- 2 tablespoons baking powder
- ½ teaspoon baking soda
- 2 teaspoons cinnamon
- 1 cup skim milk
- ½ cup nonfat plain yogurt
- 1 16-ounce can whole kernel corn with liquid
- 2 egg whites
- 1 tablespoon corn oil

MAKES 4 SERVINGS

*P*repare the cranberry butter by combining all of the butter ingredients in a food processor. Purée until the cranberries are finely chopped. Transfer the mixture to a bowl and microwave on high until the butter and sugar melt, about 3 to 6 minutes. Cool and refrigerate. The butter will thicken in a few hours when cool.

To prepare the griddle cakes, combine all of the pancake ingredients in a large mixing bowl. Stir until well blended. Scoop the batter onto a hot griddle, forming 3-inch diameter cakes. Cook until bubbles appear and sides begin to dry. Turn the cakes over and cook until golden. Serve with the butter.

— THE CAPTAIN FREEMAN INN

*S*tart your own minifarm market. Top two sawhorses with a thick piece of plywood and cover them with a quilt or checkered cloth. Arrange baskets of your garden's bounty and don't make any more excuses for growing so much zucchini that you can't even give it away. Sell it! A day of manning the roadside stand is full of play; you'll be amazed at how many interesting people stop by and what you discover.

Sweet Potato Waffles
with Apple-Cranberry Chutney

∽∾∿

Fall is not fall without a chutney, and innkeeper Mary Lynn Tucker serves chutney for breakfast. What a combination, with sweet potatoes in the waffle batter! The chutney is a nice condiment for a number of fall dishes.

I like finding pomegranates at the market. Not only do they look great just sitting in a bowl on a harvest table, but the garnet seeds sparkle like jewels when sprinkled as garnish for fall breakfasts. Whole pomegranates dry nicely and last all year as a reminder of the season's gifts.

LEFT: A FAVORITE GUEST ROOM OVERLOOKING THE GARDEN OF THE MANOR AT TAYLOR'S STORE

Sweet Potato Waffles with Apple-Cranberry Chutney (continued)

Chutney	
2	cups peeled and chopped red apples of choice
1	cup fresh cranberries (³/₄ cup dried)
¹/₄	cup golden raisins
2	tablespoons brown sugar
1	tablespoon grated orange peel
2	tablespoons cider vinegar
¹/₄	teaspoon ground cloves
¹/₄	teaspoon nutmeg
¹/₄	teaspoon cinnamon

Waffles	
³/₄	cup peeled, cooked, and mashed sweet potatoes (about ¹/₂ pound raw)
1¹/₂	teaspoons canola oil
1	egg white, slightly beaten
³/₄	cup skim milk
¹/₂	cup whole-wheat flour
1	teaspoon baking powder
¹/₄	teaspoon salt

MAKES 4 SERVINGS

*I*n a medium saucepan, combine all of the chutney ingredients. Place over high heat and bring to a boil, stirring constantly. Reduce the heat and simmer, uncovered, for about 15 minutes or until the apples are tender. Remove from the heat and allow the mixture to cool. Transfer to a food processor and pulse a few times until well combined. Keep warm.

Preheat a waffle iron. In a medium bowl combine cooled sweet potatoes, oil, egg white, and milk. Beat until blended. Add the flour, baking powder, and salt. Stir until smooth. Coat the waffle iron lightly with cooking oil spray. Ladle batter into the waffle iron in ¹/₄ cup measures. Cook until done. Serve with the chutney.

—THE MANOR AT TAYLOR'S STORE

LEFT: THE MANOR AT TAYLOR'S STORE, SMITH MOUNTAIN LAKE, VIRGINIA

Butternut Squash and Apple-Filled Tortellini with Black Currant Sage Sauce

∽∘∾

Tortellini is made here of a roasted red pepper dough. It is easy to do, but make a little extra, just in case you need to get the knack of shaping the pasta. Leave it to the creative kitchen at the Benbow to develop an autumn pasta! You will find an assortment of pasta flavors at some farm markets— usually when they sell milk and eggs, but I doubt you'll find a pasta like this one.

Tortellini

2	large red bell peppers, roasted and seeded
2	tablespoons olive oil
1	egg
2	cups all-purpose flour

Filling

2	tablespoons olive oil
1	medium yellow onion, peeled and diced
1	Granny Smith apple, cored and coarsely diced
1	Anaheim chile, seeded and diced, optional
1	butternut squash, peeled, seeded, and diced
1	tablespoon salt
$^{1}/_{2}$	teaspoon freshly cracked pepper
2	teaspoons chopped fresh sage
1	egg
$^{1}/_{2}$	cup breadcrumbs

Sauce

1	cup black currants
1	tablespoon minced shallots
1	tablespoon chopped fresh sage
2	cups dry white wine
$^{1}/_{2}$	cup maple syrup
$^{1}/_{4}$	cup brown sugar
$^{1}/_{2}$	cup (1 stick) unsalted butter
	Salt and freshly cracked pepper

*B*egin by preparing the tortellini. Purée the peppers and olive oil in a food processor until smooth. Add the egg and flour, pulsing until well mixed. Continue processing until a ball of dough forms. Turn the dough onto a floured surface and knead for 8 to 10 minutes. Cover with plastic wrap and let rest for 30 minutes.

Preheat the oven to 350°. To prepare the filling, heat the olive oil in a large oven-proof skillet. Add the onion, apple, chile, squash, salt, pepper, and sage. Cook for 5 or 6 minutes over medium-high heat. Cover the skillet with foil and bake for 30 minutes. Remove the pan from the oven and stir the stuffing ingredients until well mixed. Re-cover the dish and continue to bake for another 15 minutes or until the vegetables are tender. Allow the mixture to cool, then stir in the egg and breadcrumbs and finish the tortellini.

Roll the dough onto a floured surface to ⅛-inch thickness. Cut into 20 (3-inch squares. Set aside. Place a generous tablespoon of the filling at the corner of each pasta square). Take the bottom corner and fold up and over the filling, about two-thirds up the diamond. Press it into the pasta. Next, roll the filling toward the top of the diamond while pressing the pasta on both sides of the filling to seal. Place the dough around your index finger with filling against your nail and pull together gently. Press together. Set the tortellini aside on a lightly floured surface.

Bring a large pot of water to a boil. Drop in the tortellini, a few at a time. Cook until barely tender, about 4 to 6 minutes. Drain and keep warm.

For the sauce, combine the currants, shallots, sage, wine, maple syrup, and sugar in a saucepan over medium-high heat.

Bring to a boil. Cook, uncovered, until the volume is reduced to 1 ½ cups. Swirl in the butter and season with salt and pepper. Serve over the tortellini.

—BENBOW INN

The Soup
Kettle

Sherried Butternut Squash and Leek Soup

ৎ৵০৵ও

The combination of the nutty, buttery flavor from the squash and the tangy taste of the leeks provides a traditional fall soup. I like innkeeper/chef Claudia Ryan's easy method for preparing the butternut squash.

Picture facing chapter opener: Butternut Squash Soup, recipe on page 20

1	(2 ½ to 3-pound) butternut squash	4	sprigs fresh Italian parsley
¼	cup (½ stick) butter	4	turns of freshly cracked pepper
2	pounds (6 cups) leeks, white parts with a portion of green tops, cut into 1-inch pieces	1	cup milk
		¼	teaspoon nutmeg, more for garnish
2	whole medium cloves garlic, peeled	⅓	cup dry sherry
5	cups vegetable broth		Salt
1	cup dry white wine		Plain yogurt or sour cream for garnish
3	sprigs fresh thyme (or 1/4 teaspoon dried)		

MAKES 8 SERVINGS

*P*ierce squash with a fork and place in the microwave. Cook the squash on high for about 10 minutes (turn halfway through so squash tenderizes evenly). Peel and remove seeds. Cut the squash into medium chunks. Set aside.

Melt the butter in a large soup kettle. Add the leeks and the garlic and cook covered over medium heat about 15 minutes, stirring occasionally, until the vegetables are tender. Add the squash, 4 cups of the broth, white wine, thyme, parsley, and pepper. Cover. Over medium heat bring to a rolling boil. Stir, then simmer until the squash is soft, about 1 hour. Uncover and let cool.

Purée the soup in batches in a food processor or blender. Return the soup to the pot on low-to-medium heat. Stir in the milk, nutmeg, and sherry. Season with salt and pepper to taste. Add the extra cup of vegetable broth to thin the soup, if desired. Garnish with a teaspoon or so of yogurt or sour cream and a light sprinkle of nutmeg.

—WINDFLOWER INN

Curried Corn and Acorn Squash Soup

Hearty flavors and fresh crisp vegtables warm the palate on a cold day. Serve with a salad of Romaine and dark green-and-red lettuce and this soup will have friends begging for the recipe. To remove fresh corn kernels, slide a knife down the corncobs; or to yield the full kernels, dig up clumps of kernels with a fork.

2	cups grated carrots		1	teaspoon dried thyme or 2 teaspoons fresh thyme
2	medium onions, finely chopped		2	bay leaves
3	cups coarsely grated acorn squash		1/2	teaspoon freshly cracked pepper
1	cup coarsely grated rutabaga		2	tablespoons fresh chopped parsley
8	cups chicken stock (home-made preferred)		2	cups fresh corn kernels
2	teaspoons curry powder			Salt

MAKES 8 TO 10 SERVINGS

Combine all the ingredients except the corn and salt into a large soup pot. Bring the mixture to a boil and simmer for 5 minutes or so, just until the vegetables are tender. Add the corn and simmer for an additional 5 minutes. Pour half of the mixture into a food processor, purée, and return to the pot. Remove the bay leaves. Season with salt to taste and serve warm.

—THE WHITE OAK INN

LEFT: THE SOUP TAKES CENTER STAGE IN THE WHITE OAK INN'S GREAT ROOM.

Sweet Potato and Caramelized Apple Soup

⟨∼∞∼⟩

Primarily composed of naturally sweet ingredients, this meal-starter is the essence of autumn with its contrast of spices and savories.

Cinnamon sticks add a capricious touch. Serve with a wedge of Jarlsberg cheese and garden greens and you have lunch. The great smell coming from your kitchen as you cook this dish will transport you to this inn, another that you must visit once in your lifetime.

Top your pumpkin pie with edible fall leaves. Make the leaves out of pastry dough, cut freehand (include marks for veins) or with the aid of a real leaf. Bake in the oven (they may curl a bit but will be all the more natural that way) and place as a garnish on the pie or with a slice of pie.

2	tablespoons butter	1/4	teaspoon nutmeg
1	teaspoon chopped garlic	1 1/2	teaspoons salt
1	medium onion, cut into medium dice	1/4	teaspoon freshly cracked pepper
2	stalks celery, cut into medium dice	1	Granny Smith apple, cut into 1/2-inch dice
1	leek, white part only, cut into 1-inch pieces	1 1/4	cups apple cider
1 1/2	pounds sweet potatoes, peeled and cut into 1-inch chunks	3	tablespoons dark molasses
		1	cup heavy cream
5	cups chicken stock	8	fresh mint sprigs
18	3-inch cinnamon sticks		

MAKES 8 SERVINGS

In a large stockpot, melt 1 tablespoon of the butter and add the garlic, onion, celery, and leek, cooking just until lightly browned. Add the potatoes, chicken stock, 2 of the cinnamon sticks, nutmeg, and salt and pepper to taste. Simmer the mixture until the potatoes are tender, 15 to 20 minutes. Purée the mixture in a food processor until smooth. Keep warm.

Meanwhile, caramelize the apples. Heat the remaining butter in a skillet and add the diced apple. Sauté a few seconds and add 1/4 cup of the apple cider. Heat through and toss until apples are well coated. Set aside.

Stir the molasses into the stockpot, then the remaining 1 cup of the cider, the cream, and the caramelized apple. Raise the heat and cook for a few minutes until warmed through. Remove the cinnamon sticks and discard. Garnish with fresh sticks crisscrossed in the center of the soup, and top with a sprig of mint.

—THE INN AT BLACKBERRY FARM

Pear and Cinnamon Rosemary Soup

∽∾∾

Leftovers of this delicious soup may be served by the fire in clear mugs as an appetizer. Although the heavy cream is divided among 10 servings, you may prefer to substitute light cream. Elegance at the edge of a forest describes the charms of Windham Hill. I remember enjoying this soup from a garden-view table overlooking the grassy meadow . . . Oh, where is my journal? . . .

12	ripe pears		2	cinnamon sticks
1/4	cup peanut oil		2	large sprigs fresh rosemary (2 teaspoons dried)
1	medium onion, coarsely chopped		2	cups heavy cream
2	cups pear or other slightly fruity wine		1	teaspoon cinnamon
1	quart low-fat chicken stock or broth			Sour cream for garnish
				Nutmeg for garnish

MAKES 10 SERVINGS

Peel, core, and coarsely chop the pears. Set aside.

In a large nonstick skillet heat the oil and sauté the onion over medium–high heat until wilted. Add the pears, the wine, and the stock. Tie the cinnamon sticks and the rosemary in a double layer of cheesecloth and add to the skillet. Bring the mixture to a boil, then simmer for 20 minutes. Remove the spice bag and transfer the mixture in batches to a food processor. Process until puréed. Return the mixture to the skillet and add the cream and the cinnamon. For garnish, add a teaspoon or so of sour cream and a sprinkle of nutmeg.

—WINDHAM HILL INN

LEFT: AUTUMN SCENE AT A DRIED FLOWER, PRODUCE MARKET, AND GIFT SHOP IN HAGERSTOWN, MARYLAND CALLED HOMEPLACE EVERLASTINGS. ONE OF MY FAVORITE SIMPLE PLEASURES IS MY VISIT HERE EVERY FALL.

Onion and Black Bean Soup

∽○∽

 I will never forget savoring this soup on a cold Montana night in front of a fire, with Elizabeth Turney's crusty homemade bread, and later experiencing the hot tub on the deck in below-zero temperatures, while gazing, without a care, at the tall pines, the full moon, and Venus.

A plain glass of hot apple cider is delicious with an old-fashioned, powdered sugar doughnut; or make our apple-cider doughnuts on page 92.

2	pounds dried black beans		2	stalks celery, chopped
2	quarts water or chicken stock		1	tablespoon lemon juice
2	bay leaves		1/4	cup dry sherry
1/2	(small) bunch cilantro			Salt and freshly cracked pepper
2	ham hocks			
4	jalapeño peppers, seeded			Sour cream or plain yogurt
2	tablespoons olive oil		1	lemon, sliced into thin rounds, for garnish
2	cloves garlic, diced			
2	onions, coarsely chopped			Chopped cilantro for garnish
2	large carrots, coarsely chopped			

MAKES 8 TO 10 SERVINGS

Rinse the beans and cover them with water. Soak for at least 4 hours or overnight. Drain the beans and transfer them to a stockpot with the water. Add the bay leaves, cilantro, ham hocks, peppers, olive oil, garlic, onions, carrots, and celery. Simmer over low heat for 1¹/₂ hours.

Discard the bay leaves and ham hocks. Transfer the cooked ingredients to a food processor, allowing the liquid to remain in the pot. Purée and return to the stockpot. Mix the purée and broth until thoroughly combined. Stir in the lemon juice and sherry. Season with salt and pepper. Serve with a dollop of sour cream or yogurt and garnish with lemon slices and sprinkles of cilantro.

—BEAR CREEK LODGE

Homemade Breads

Michael Carnahan's Basic Bread Recipe

⋖◦⋗

Watching the chef bake bread, is like watching a master create. I wanted to sit for hours as Chef Michael Carnahan kneaded and twisted breads into shape with a loving, poetic hand. Take your time with this easy bread and consider it not a task but a simple pleasure. Form the breads into rounds, braids, or bake in a loaf pan. Bread is the essence of cooking at this fine country inn where the centers of attention are the kitchen and dining in the gardens as the sun sets. Add 2 finely chopped tablespoonfuls of a favorite fresh herb if desired.

5	cups all-purpose flour, plus 1 cup more		2	tablespoons sugar
			3	tablespoons active dry yeast
2	eggs		1	tablespoon salt
2	tablespoons butter, softened		1³/₄	cups warm water (110° to 115°)

In the large bowl of an electric mixer, add all of the ingredients except the 1 cup more of flour. Mix the dough until the butter is melted and worked into the dough (about 3 minutes). Remove the beaters from the mixer and add the dough hook and the last cup of flour. Run the mixer on medium speed for about 7 minutes, at which point the dough should be smooth and elastic. Turn the dough out into an oiled bowl. Cover the bowl and let the dough rise in a warm, draft-free place until doubled in size. Punch the dough down and cut into 3 equal portions. Roll each piece of dough out into the shape of a loaf and set into a 9x5-inch loaf pan. (Twist into a braid or shape into a round if not shaping into a loaf and then place on a baking sheet.) Let the dough rise again for about an hour or until it has doubled in size. Brush the dough with a little beaten egg and bake in a 400° oven for 18 to 20 minutes or until golden brown.

—INN AT CEDAR FALLS

PICTURE FACING CHAPTER OPENER: BREADS IN A LOG CABIN AT THE INN AT CEDAR FALLS

LEFT: CEDAR FALLS, LOGAN, OHIO

Cheddar Cheese and Wine Bread

꿍

Here's the traditional snack of cheese and wine in one wonderful loaf. A non-yeast bread, this easy recipe is a savory addition to a salad and is great in a picnic hamper with other goodies for a fall outing. We took it down to the caves and waterfalls of the Hocking Hills area—a region not to be missed.

1	cup plus 2 tablespoons all-purpose flour	1	teaspoon minced onion
		1	egg, beaten
$1/2$	teaspoon baking powder	$1/4$	cup whole milk
$1/4$	teaspoon cream of tartar	$1/4$	cup dry white wine
$1/2$	teaspoon salt	1	teaspoon each: finely chopped basil, parsley, chives
$1/8$	teaspoon baking soda		
$1/4$	cup nonfat dry milk	$1/4$	cup freshly grated sharp cheddar cheese (or 3 tablespoons Parmesan cheese)
$1/3$	cup vegetable shortening		
1	tablespoon sugar		

MAKES 8 SERVINGS

*P*reheat the oven to 425°. In a large bowl sift together the flour, baking powder, cream of tartar, salt, baking soda, and dry milk. Add the shortening, rubbing it in with your fingers until it forms coarse crumbs.

In a separate small bowl, combine the sugar, onion, egg, milk, white wine, and herbs. Gently fold this into the crumbs. Spread the batter into a greased and lightly floured 8-inch round cake pan. Bake 15 minutes or until the bread begins to turn golden. Remove the pan from the oven and sprinkle the grated cheese evenly over the bread. Bake for an additional 5 minutes or until the cheese has melted. Allow the bread to cool for about 15 minutes before serving.

Slice into wedges while still slightly warm.

—THE INN AT CEDAR FALLS

RIGHT: CHEDDAR CHEESE AND WINE BREAD

Apple Butter Bread

∽∾

When you cook up a country fall supper, this comforting yeast bread, with a touch of sweetness and the surprise of apple butter inside, is bound to complement almost anything else you prepare. This bread goes nicely with the Curried Corn and Acorn Squash Soup on page 23. Crane House makes and sells its own apple butter.

Bread		Filling	
1/2	cup (1 stick) margarine, softened	1	cup unsweetened or lightly sweetened apple butter
2	cups lukewarm water	1/2	cup firmly packed brown sugar
1	small package quick-acting yeast		
6	cups all-purpose flour		
1/3	cup sugar		

MAKES 2 LOAVES

In the large bowl of an electric mixer, stir together the margarine and water. Add the yeast, flour, and sugar. Combine the mixture with a dough hook for at least 3 or 4 minutes. Place a tea towel over the bowl and let the dough rest for 15 minutes. Punch the dough down again, working it for about 1 minute.

Preheat the oven to 350°. On a heavily floured board cut the dough in 2 equal pieces. Roll each piece into a 7x15-inch rectangle. Evenly divide the apple butter and then the brown sugar overtop the dough. Roll up each piece jellyroll style, rolling tightly. Place each loaf in a lightly greased 9x5-inch loaf pan. Cover each with a tea towel and let rise until doubled in bulk, about 35 minutes. Bake for 35 to 40 minutes or until golden brown.

—CRANE HOUSE B&B

Here's a recipe that makes syrup from apple cider for pancakes, waffles, or French toast: In a nonstick saucepan, cook until boiling, 2 cups apple cider, 1/2 stick butter, 2 tablespoons lemon juice with 1 cup of sugar, 1 teaspoon cinnamon, and 3 tablespoons biscuit mix. Boil, stirring for 1 minute or until syrup is smooth and thickened. Makes 3 cups. Thanks to Trisha's B&B in Jackson, Missouri.

Sweet Potato Bread

❦

Although this is a sweet bread, it is versatile and can be served as either a dinner or a breakfast bread. The bread's flavor is further enhanced with a serving of leftover cranberry butter found with the griddle cakes recipe on page 10.

Bittersweet is a favorite autumn find at the market. Buy whatever there is (usually it's not much). The more you have, the more ways you'll find to entwine it among fall centerpieces or just wiggle it around a casserole when serving at the table.

1	cup (2 sticks) butter, softened	1	teaspoon cinnamon
2	cups sugar	$1/2$	teaspoon nutmeg
4	eggs	$1/4$	teaspoon salt
$2 1/2$	cups (about 2 large potatoes) peeled, cooked, and mashed sweet potatoes	1	teaspoon vanilla extract
		$1/2$	cup unsweetened flaked coconut
3	cups all-purpose flour	$1/2$	cup chopped pecans
2	teaspoons baking powder		
1	teaspoon baking soda		

MAKES 8 TO 10 SERVINGS

*P*reheat the oven to 350°. In a large mixing bowl cream the butter, then gradually beat in the sugar. When it is smooth, beat in the eggs, one at a time. Add the sweet potatoes and continue to beat.

In a medium bowl, combine the flour, baking powder, baking soda, cinnamon, nutmeg, and salt. Slowly add the dry ingredients to the sweet potato mixture, beating after each addition. At this point the batter will become stiff. Stir in the vanilla, coconut, and nuts.

Pour the batter into a well-greased 10-inch tube pan and bake for 1 hour and 15 minutes or until a tester comes clean. Cool the bread for 15 minutes before removing from the pan, then cool completely.

—MAPLEWOOD INN

Pumpkin Cornbread

The flavor of a recipe calling for cornmeal is enhanced when you use stoneground meal. I order such grains from Nora Mill Granary in Sautee, Georgia (1-800-927-2375), where they grind corn and wheat between centuries-old grindstones. The rich ground-corn taste with the pumpkin and cranberry makes this a very special bread but remember, it is a cornbread and will be denser than a sweet, quick bread.

1¼	cups stoneground cornmeal	3	eggs
1½	cups sifted all-purpose flour	1	cup cooked pumpkin
1	teaspoon cinnamon	8	ounces whole-berry cranberry sauce
½	teaspoon mace (optional)	²⁄₃	cup chopped pecans
1½	teaspoons salt		
½	teaspoon baking powder		
¼	cup (½ stick) butter, plus 2 tablespoons		

MAKES 8 SERVINGS

*P*reheat the oven to 350°. Grease and flour a 9x5-inch loaf pan. In a medium bowl, mix together the cornmeal and the flour. Add the cinnamon, mace, salt, and baking powder. Set aside.

In a large bowl of an electric mixer, cream together the butter and eggs. Add the pumpkin and the cranberry sauce. Blend in the dry ingredients and fold in the pecans, mixing just until moistened. Pour the batter into the prepared pan. Bake for about 1 hour or until a tester comes clean and the bread is golden brown.

—LEDFORD MILL AND MUSEUM

While at the market, ask a farmer if you can schedule a hayride through his fields. Rally a group of friends and offer a fee for the farmer's labor.

Fig 'n' Fruit Whole Wheat Bread

౾ఄ౾

I jump at the chance to make a recipe using figs. This sweet and nutritious bread is served at the inn around holiday time. Figs provide lots of iron and calcium. They were an early symbol of peace and prosperity and there are hundreds of varieties. The Calimyrna, with a greenish appearance, is one of the more common. Figs start showing up in farmers markets in the fall. The innkeeper has a cookbook, *Heart Healthy Hospitality*. But everything in this little inn is served with heart-felt hospitality.

Have an old-fashioned pie swap. Ask everyone to bring a homemade pie or autumn fruit tart and sample, sample, sample.

LEFT: THE KITCHEN OF THE MANOR AT TAYLOR'S STORE

THE MANOR AT TAYLOR'S STORE

There's nothing like summer stock theater. We used to make it to the shows at the Cider Mill Playhouse every fall. There's something about plays and autumn that go together. Ask about a play in town when you reserve your room at an inn.

1	cup dried Calimyrna figs	1	egg
1	cup dried apricots	1	teaspoon grated lemon zest
1	cup golden raisins	1	cup all-purpose flour
1	cup pitted dates	1	cup whole-wheat pastry flour
1½	cups water	2	teaspoons baking powder
¼	cup margarine	1	teaspoon baking soda
¾	cup sugar	1	teaspoon salt

MAKES 2 LOAVES

*C*oat 2 9x5-inch loaf pans with cooking oil spray. Place the figs, apricots, raisins, and dates in a small saucepan with the water. Cover and simmer for 5 minutes. Drain, reserving ⅔ cup liquid. Cool. Chop the fruits into a medium dice. Set aside.

In a large bowl place the margarine, sugar, egg, and lemon zest and beat with an electric hand mixer until smooth and creamy. In a medium bowl, use a fork to combine the flours, baking powder, baking soda, and salt. Sift this into the sugar-and-lemon mixture. Fold in the fruit. Stir in the reserved fruit liquid and mix with the fork until blended. Spoon the batter into the loaf pans. Preheat the oven to 350°. Let the pan stand for 15 minutes, then bake for 45 minutes or until a tester inserted comes clean.

—THE MANOR AT TAYLOR'S STORE

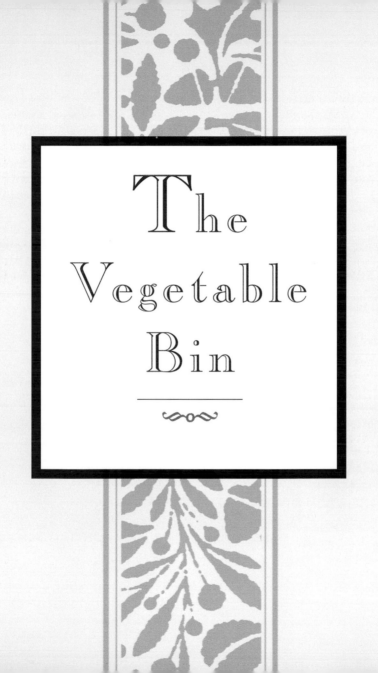

The Vegetable Bin

Sunflower Salad

୦୦

Once upon a time, Dorry Norris ran Sage Cottage, a bed-and-breakfast in Trumansburg, New York. Dorry is one of America's foremost herbalists. She orchestrated this salad to which I have added roasted red peppers, purple cabbage, and soft, buttery lettuce. Although sunflowers are not edible, their seeds certainly are, so I bow to Dorry for inspiring this salad to grace an early harvest table.

3/4	cup sunflower seeds, lightly toasted	1	red pepper, roasted and sliced julienne
2	tablespoons sunflower oil	1/2	small head purple (red) cabbage, sliced julienne
1/2	cup apple cider vinegar		
2	medium cloves garlic, minced	2	small yellow squash, sliced into 1/8-inch rounds
	Freshly cracked pepper		
1	head butter or Boston lettuce	2	small zucchini, grated

MAKES 6 SERVINGS

In a blender, whirl together 1/4 cup of the seeds, the oil, vinegar, garlic, and a few twists of cracked black pepper. Set aside.

Arrange a few lettuce leaves on each serving plate. Add the red pepper to the center of each plate. Place the cabbage around the plate topped by the yellow squash rounds. Add the grated zucchini and pour the dressing over all. Sprinkle with the reserved sunflower seeds. Chill for 30 minutes in the refrigerator before serving.

—GAIL'S KITCHEN

The tops of pies can be enriched by glazes. Fruit juices will yield a slight taste and offer a warm glow. Milk will darken the top to a rich brown. An egg wash of 1 egg beaten with 1 tablespoon of milk will make the top golden and glossy. Unglazed pie crusts may also be dusted with powdered sugar. Dust after the pie has cooled.

Baked Indian Chowder Gratin

I enjoy this as an entrée with a salad and bread, but it is most popularly served as a side dish, either as a quiche dish or in individual custard cups. The chefs at the Governor's Inn combine tradition with creative cuisine. This recipe is one example from one of America's most impressive inn menus. In our test kitchen, we also browned the top just before serving for color. Either way, it's delicious.

1/2	cup (1 stick) butter	2 1/2	cups chablis
5	leeks, well trimmed and coarsely chopped	1	cup dry sherry
1/4	cup all-purpose flour	1/2	cup chicken stock
	Kernels cut from 12 cars of corn	1/8	teaspoon white pepper
		1/8	teaspoon allspice
2	cups cooked pumpkin	1/2	pound lean maple bacon
1	quart light cream	6	slices Cheddar cheese

MAKES 6 SERVINGS

*M*elt the butter in a large soup pot. Add all of the ingredients except the bacon and Cheddar cheese. Simmer for about 15 minutes. While simmering, fry the bacon. Drain and chop into small pieces.

When the chowder ingredients are cooked and tender, transfer half of the mixture to a blender and purée until smooth. Pour the purée into the bacon pan and simmer for about 5 minutes, just enough to pick up the flavor of the bacon. Stir the purée back into the soup pot. Add the bacon and simmer for 30 minutes. Preheat the oven to 400°. Evenly divide the chowder into 6 oven-proof soup bowls or bake in a quiche dish. Top each dish with a slice of cheddar cheese. Bake for 30 minutes or until cheese is melted. Cook longer to brown or place under broiler for a few minutes. Serve bubbling hot.

—THE GOVERNOR'S INN

The temptation is great to buy several jugs full of apple cider at the farmers market. Buy with abandon. A tip from Hampshire House 1884 in Romney, West Virginia, explains that you can freeze the cider and it will taste just as fresh when it is thawed. Leave room for expansion in the jug.

Roasted Butternut Squash and Red Pepper Pizza with Nutmeg Sauce and Cornmeal Crust

✎

The inspiration for this recipe came from refrigerated pizza dough that was expiring, red farm peppers I had roasted and frozen during the summer, and a few fresh-dough pizza recipes from *Gourmet* magazine. The pizza has a milk-and-cheese sauce base. I have another one for fall that you must try. It tops a pizza shell with thinly sliced red apples, ground Italian sweet sausage, shredded Cheddar cheese, and a few roasted peppers.

1	(1 3/4 to 2 pounds) butternut squash, peeled, seeded, and cut into 1/2-inch cubes	
1	teaspoon sunflower oil	
	Salt and freshly cracked pepper	

Sauce

1 1/2	cups whole milk
2	tablespoons all-purpose flour
1/2	teaspoon grated nutmeg
	Salt

Pizza

1	teaspoon yellow cornmeal
	Fresh dough to make 1 16x12-inch pizza or refrigerated rolled pizza dough
1	cup grated Asiago cheese
2	large red bell peppers, roasted and cut julienne
1	tablespoon chopped fresh rosemary
2	large cloves garlic, minced
	Sprigs of rosemary for garnish

MAKES 1 16X12-INCH PIZZA

*P*reheat the oven to 450°. In a large bowl toss the squash with the oil and salt and pepper. Place squash in a baking dish and roast for about 15 minutes, turning once and baking for another 15 minutes or until golden brown. Remove from the pan and set aside.

In a medium saucepan over medium heat, stir together the milk and the flour until incorporated. Add the nutmeg and cook for another 2 minutes. Add salt to taste. Raise the oven temperature to 500°.

Sprinkle 1 teaspoon of the cornmeal onto a work surface. Roll out the pizza dough into a 12x16-inch oval and transfer to a nonstick baking sheet. Repeat with the remaining dough. (Note: you can make a round pizza if desired.)

Spread the sauce over the pizza, leaving a 1/2-inch border around the edge. Sprinkle with the Asiago cheese, squash, peppers, rosemary, and garlic. Season with black pepper to taste. Bake the pizza for 15 minutes or until the crust is crisp and golden. Garnish with sprigs of rosemary.

—GAIL'S KITCHEN

Rutabaga and Potato Maple Purée

⋙⋘

To rejuvenate winter vegetables, rally round the rutabaga, as Tony Clark did at the inn. This makes a great side dish for meat or poultry and allows you to broaden your fall harvest basket.

4	cups water		3	tablespoons unsalted butter
2	medium white potatoes, peeled and cut into large chunks		1	tablespoon pure maple syrup
			1	tablespoon dry sherry
1	small rutabaga, peeled and cut into large chunks			Salt and freshly cracked pepper
1/2	teaspoon salt			

MAKES 4 SERVINGS

In a large saucepan bring the water to a boil. Add the potatoes, rutabaga, and salt and cook over medium-high heat for about 30 minutes or until the vegetables are tender. Drain the vegetables. Let them cool.

Transfer the cooled vegetables to a food processor. Add the butter, syrup, and sherry and process until blended. Do not overmix. Return the mixture to the pot. Cook over medium low heat for about 10 minutes, stirring occasionally. Season with salt and pepper.

—BLUEBERRY HILL

While on your way to an inn, stop whenever you see a maple syrup sign. Once a farmer invited me into the kitchen to sample syrup grades. The maple syrup stop led to a tour of the family farm. What a day!

S*wiss Chard with Pecans*

∾०∾

Although in the beet family, Swiss chard or chard is prepared and used similarly to spinach. The vegetable is rich in iron and vitamins A and C. A hearty, fulfilling vegetable, it is comforting on a cold autumn day.

3	tablespoons unsalted butter		Freshly grated nutmeg
3	tablespoons pecans, coarsely chopped	1/4	teaspoon salt
			Freshly cracked pepper
3	pounds fresh Swiss chard		

MAKES 6 TO 8 SERVINGS

In a small skillet, heat 1 tablespoon of the butter and sauté the pecans over moderate heat until they are golden. Set aside to drain on absorbent towels.

Wash the Swiss chard well to remove any grit. Do not dry. Remove the coarse main stem. In a large skillet, cook the chard over medium-high heat in the water that still clings to the leaves after washing. When the chard wilts, add the remaining butter, the pecans, and a grating of fresh nutmeg. Season with salt and pepper. Heat through and serve.

—THE FEARRINGTON HOUSE

TAKING TIME OUT FOR TEA ON THE PORCH OF THE INN AT OLDE NEW BERLIN AFTER
SHOPPING FOR RECIPE INGREDIENTS USED IN THE SQUASH TARTS ON PAGE 59

Mushroom and Cheese Filled Squash Tarts

soos

Stuffed with vegetables and topped with cheese, this dish is a meal in one. The inn offers this as one of its vegetarian entrées.

2	medium acorn squash, seeded and cut in half	1	teaspoon basil
	Olive oil for sautéing	1	teaspoon oregano
2¹/₂	cups assorted fresh vegetables, cut into a medium dice (broccoli, cauliflower, zucchini, summer squash, snow peas, scallions)	1	teaspoon thyme
		1	cup dry white wine
		¹/₄	cup fresh lime juice
		¹/₈	teaspoon salt
		¹/₂	teaspoon freshly cracked pepper
1	carrot, cut into medium dice	2 to 3	tablespoons light brown sugar
4	medium button mushrooms, thinly sliced	8	ounces Gouda cheese, grated

MAKES 4 SERVINGS

Steam the squash until crisp tender. Set aside. Preheat the oven to 350°. In a large skillet heat the oil and sauté the assorted vegetables, carrots, and mushrooms over medium-high heat for about 5 minutes or until al dente. Stir in the basil, oregano, thyme, wine, and lime juice. Simmer for 3 to 4 minutes. Season with salt and pepper.

Coat the inside of each squash half with brown sugar. Place them in a microwave for 1 to 2 minutes, just enough to warm slightly. Fill the squash with the sautéed vegetable mixture and top with the Gouda cheese. Bake for 15 minutes or until heated through and the cheese is melted. Serve immediately.

—THE INN AT OLDE NEW BERLIN

Eggplant and Zucchini Stuffed with Rice and Tomatoes

〜∘〜

The ghost-like white eggplants appear in the fall and I love their slightly piquant, slightly sweet flavors. I make the inn's recipe with this variety, but the dark purple eggplant also works fine.

4	small-to-medium eggplants	3	tablespoons mixed fresh herbs (parsley, marjoram, chives), minced
1/3	cup olive oil		
4	small zucchini	1/2	teaspoon salt
10	ounces frozen spinach		Freshly cracked pepper
4	ounces cherry tomatoes	1/2	cup Parmesan cheese, freshly grated
2	medium onions, finely chopped		
2	cloves garlic, minced		
1	cup raw rice, cooked		

MAKES 8 SERVINGS

*P*reheat the oven to 400°. Cut the eggplants in half lengthwise. Leaving the flesh intact, cut around the edge of the eggplant to leave a 1/4-inch wall. Place face down in a pan that has been drizzled with 2 tablespoons of the olive oil. Bake for about 10 minutes or until the flesh is slightly soft and browned.

Cut the zucchini in the same fashion as the eggplant and brown in 2 tablespoons of the olive oil in the oven for about 10 minutes or until the flesh is lightly softened. Scoop out the pulp of both vegetables. Chop the pulp coarsely and reserve.

Cook the frozen spinach in boiling water about 4 to 5 minutes or just until it separates. Refresh under cold water and drain. Gather the spinach in small amounts and squeeze by the handful until very dry. Chop coarsely and set aside.

Cut the cherry tomatoes in half. Scrape the seeds from the pulp and discard. Chop the tomatoes coarsely and set aside.

In a large skillet, cook the onions with the garlic in 1 tablespoon of the olive oil for about 5 minutes over medium heat until they are translucent but not browned. Add the reserved eggplant and zucchini pulp and continue to cook for 5 to 10 minutes.

Add the spinach, tomatoes, rice, and herbs, mixing to incorporate. Season with salt and pepper to taste. Divide the mixture among the vegetable shells. Sprinkle Parmesan cheese overtop and drizzle with the remaining olive oil. Bake in the same oven for 10 minutes or until slightly brown.

—THE FEARRINGTON HOUSE

*M*edley of Caramel Carrots, Turnips, and Chestnuts

꼬꼬

Chestnuts arrive at some farm markets in September, but they are available in supermarkets through the holidays. Choose nuts that are firm and plump and free of blemishes. The inn's recipe calls for either fresh or canned. If using fresh nuts, make slits on the tops of the nuts to prevent bursting and roast in the oven at 350° in a pan filled with about $1/4$ inch of water for about 15 minutes or until heated through and tender.

$1/2$	pound carrots, peeled		$1/4$	cup chestnuts (fresh-cooked or canned)
$1/2$	pound turnips, peeled			Freshly grated nutmeg
1	tablespoon butter			
$1/4$	cup firmly packed brown sugar			

MAKES 6 SERVINGS

*S*lice carrots and turnips into $1/8$-inch rounds. Cook in boiling salted water until crisp tender. Refresh under cold running water.

Melt the butter in a medium skillet and add the brown sugar, carrots, and turnips. Toss vegetables and coat well. Cook until the brown sugar has dissolved and has made a glaze for the vegetables.

Peel the chestnuts or drain them if using canned. Cut them julienne and add them to the pan to heat through. Grate fresh nutmeg overtop the vegetables and mix before serving.

—THE FEARRINGTON HOUSE

LEFT: MY FAVORITE SECRET PLACE FROM WHICH TO VIEW THE COLORS

Yam and Apple Casserole

✎

Yams are full of antioxidant vitamins. Served along with a chicken, turkey, or simply by themselves, you won't have any leftovers from this dish. The inn with its log cabins and fabulous food is ever-romantic. Fall blazes with color here and there's still time to eat under candlelight on wooden tables in the garden.

2	pounds fresh yams, peeled, cut into quarters, and cooked tender (or 2 16-ounce cans, drained)	2	tablespoons dry sherry
		$3/4$	teaspoon cinnamon
		$1/8$	teaspoon salt
$1/2$	cup (1 stick) butter, melted	2	Granny Smith apples, cored, peeled, and sliced
$1/2$	cup dark corn syrup		
$1/4$	cup plus 2 tablespoons light brown sugar		

MAKES 6 TO 8 SERVINGS

*P*reheat the oven to 350°. In a food processor, purée the yams, 6 tablespoons of the butter, the syrup, sugar, sherry, cinnamon, and salt. Spread half of the mixture into a greased 10-inch pie plate. Arrange half of the apple slices overtop. Add the remaining yam purée and then apple slices. Brush the top layer of apples with the remaining 2 tablespoons of butter. Bake for about 45 minutes or until the apples are tender.

—THE INN AT CEDAR FALLS

The
Butcher's
Block

Red Flannel Hash

∽◌∽

Red Flannel Hash gets its name from the mixture of beef and potatoes that is colored by beets. It is an old-time recipe, utilizing leftovers from Sunday dinner. You may substitute fresh beets for canned. For a fall breakfast, serve the hash with a side order of eggs.

2	tablespoons butter
1/4	cup finely chopped leeks (white part only)
2	cups chopped cooked white potatoes
3/4	pound cleaned and cooked beets, sliced
1 1/2	cups corned beef chunks
	Salt and pepper
2	tablespoons milk

MAKES 4 SERVINGS

Heat the butter in a large nonstick skillet and cook the leeks until tender, about 5 minutes. Stir in the potatoes, beets, and beef. Season with salt and pepper. Cook over medium heat, stirring occasionally for 8 to 10 minutes or until browned. Stir in the milk and heat through.

—ROWELL'S INN

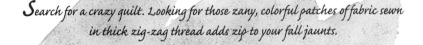

Search for a crazy quilt. Looking for those zany, colorful patches of fabric sewn in thick zig-zag thread adds zip to your fall jaunts.

Beef and Pumpkin Stew

෴

If using a fresh pumpkin, serve the stew from the pumpkin shell. A nice accompaniment is to serve the stew on individual plates on top of buttered egg noodles. This dish makes everyone smile, including the jack-o'-lanterns and sunflowers.

Corn-on-the-cob tastes good even when not cooked. Sample corn by picking off a kernel. How sweet it is! Fresh corn is evident by its light green, unwrinkled husks. Take corn home directly and refrigerate.

1	tablespoon sunflower oil	1	teaspoon fresh thyme
1½	pounds lean beef stew meat, cut into 1-inch cubes	½	teaspoon marjoram
		1	4 ½-to 5-pound pumpkin
1	large Vidalia onion, cut into medium dice	¼	cup all-purpose flour
		1	cup water
2	stalks celery, coarsely chopped	1	cup fresh-cut green beans, cut in half
1	cup stewed tomatoes, chopped		
4	cups organic vegetable broth, or more	1	carrot, coarsely diced (about ¾ cup)
¼	teaspoon salt		
½	teaspoon white pepper		

MAKES 4 SERVINGS

In a 4-quart soup pot, heat the sunflower oil and sauté the beef until browned on all sides. Add the onion and celery and cook until lightly browned. Add the tomatoes.

Stir in the broth, salt, pepper, thyme, and marjoram. Heat to boiling, then lower to medium heat and cook covered 1 hour. If the stew begins to dry up while cooking, add more broth or water ¼ cup at a time. Meanwhile, prepare the pumpkin. Remove the top of the pumpkin, placing the knife about 2 inches down from the base of the stem. Trim all around the rim of the gourd, cutting decoratively to form jagged points. Scoop out the seeds. (Dry them on a paper towel at room temperature, add some salt, and snack on them later.) Peel the pumpkin top and trimmings to yield about 2 cups of fresh pumpkin, cut into 1-inch cubes. Add the cubed pumpkin to the beef mixture after it has cooked for 1 hour. Cook 30 minutes longer, or until the pumpkin is tender.

While it is cooking, preheat the oven to 350° and bake the pumpkin shell for about 20 minutes or until warm. Stir the flour into the 1 cup of water and add it to the meat with the green beans and carrot. Cook, stirring, until the stew is thickened, about 5 or 10 minutes more. Spoon the stew into the pumpkin and serve.

—GAIL'S KITCHEN

Spiced Port-Glazed Pork Chops
with Cranberry Conserve

Rowell's is a quintessential country inn where Lee joins his wife, Beth Davis, in making the guests' dinner. This traditional New England-style recipe marries apples and orange zest with the sweetness of port for a harvest supper that is guaranteed to be memorable.

The average ear of corn has eight hundred kernels, arranged in sixteen rows.

Chops

	Approximately 1/2 cup all-purpose flour
	Salt and freshly cracked pepper
6	(1/2-inch thick) center-cut pork chops
2	tablespoons sunflower oil
2	tablespoons unsalted butter
1	medium Vidalia onion, minced
1	large Granny Smith apple, cored, pared, and thinly sliced

Glaze

3/4	cup ruby port wine
3/4	cup beef broth
1	tablespoon orange zest
1/2	teaspoon cinnamon
1/2	teaspoon freshly ground ginger
1/2	teaspoon ground cloves

Conserve

1	cup fresh cranberries
1/4	cup finely chopped pecans
1/2	cup water
1	tablespoon pure maple syrup

MAKES 6 SERVINGS

Preheat the oven to 325°. Season the flour with salt and pepper and coat the chops. In a medium skillet heat the oil and 1 tablespoon of the butter. Brown the chops for about 1 minute on each side. Arrange the chops in a 9x13-inch baking dish, overlapping the chops.

Pour off all but 2 tablespoons of the pan drippings. Add the onion and sauté until golden, about 5 minutes. Remove the onion using a slotted spoon. Add the remaining butter and apples, and sauté until golden, about 4 minutes. Remove the apples using a slotted spoon. Set aside. Add the port, broth, orange zest, and spices to the skillet, deglazing the pan. Pour the port mixture over the chops. Cover the baking dish and cook for 25 minutes, turning the chops at the half-time.

Meanwhile, in a small saucepan, bring to a boil over medium-high heat, the cranberries, pecans, water, and syrup. Reduce the heat and simmer 5 minutes.

Remove the chops from the oven and drape with the onions, apples, and cranberry conserve. Return to the oven and cook for about 5 minutes to heat through.

—ROWELL'S INN

[73]

Rosemary and Ginger Pork Tenderloin with Spiced Pear Sauce

A simple roasted pork, dressed with delicious maple flavorings and accented with a fruity cinnamon and nutmeg sauce, is great served with the yam casserole on page 64 or with wild rice and wheatberries.

Pork		Sauce	
1	(3 ½-pound) boneless pork loin	1	teaspoon olive oil
	Salt and pepper	2	pears (about 1 pound), peeled, cored, and cut into ¾-inch slices
1	tablespoon minced ginger		
1	teaspoon fresh, chopped rosemary	1	shallot, minced
		1	clove garlic, minced
1	teaspoon fresh, chopped thyme	⅓	cup dry white wine
		½	cup chicken stock
1	cup dry white wine	2	tablespoons pure maple syrup
½	cup pure maple syrup	½	teaspoon cinnamon
		¼	teaspoon ground nutmeg

MAKES 6 SERVINGS

*P*reheat the oven to 350°. Place the loin in a shallow roasting pan and season with salt, pepper, ginger, rosemary, and thyme. Pour the wine into the bottom of the pan and place in the oven. Cook for 1 hour, basting occasionally.

After 1 hour, combine the maple syrup with 3 tablespoons of pan drippings. Brush the mixture over the pork loin and return it to the oven for 30 to 45 minutes or until the temperature of the meat reaches 150° to 160°.

Meanwhile, prepare the sauce. In a heavy saucepan heat the olive oil over medium-low heat. Add the pears and sauté until golden, about 6 minutes. Stir in the shallot and garlic. Sauté until tender and translucent. Pour in the wine, chicken stock, syrup, and spices. Cover and simmer until the pears are soft, stirring occasionally. Transfer the mixture to a food processor and purée until smooth (the consistency should be that of applesauce). Add more stock to thin the sauce, if desired. Serve with the pork loin.

—THE INN AT CEDAR FALLS

Maple-Glazed Ham Rolls
with Tomato and Sweet Mustard Sauce

❧

Rowell's serves this dish as an entrée, sometimes shaping it into a meatloaf instead of individual rolls. This is a nice company-coming-for-the-weekend dish. I like this served with a slaw or sautéed red cabbage.

Rolls		Sauce	
2½	pounds ground ham of choice	2	(10 ¾-ounce) cans tomato soup
1	pound ground veal		
1½	pounds ground pork	2	teaspoons dry mustard
3	cups crushed graham crackers	¾	cup apple cider vinegar
2	cups evaporated milk	2¼	cups brown sugar
3	eggs, slightly beaten		

MAKES 6 SERVINGS

*P*reheat the oven to 350°. In a large bowl, mix together all of the ingredients and form the mixture into quenelle (egg) shapes, using about 1 cup per roll. Place into a 9x13-inch baking dish (rolls should not touch each other in the pan). Mix together all of the ingredients for the sauce. Pour the sauce all over the rolls and bake for 1 hour or until the meat is cooked through, basting with pan juices after 30 minutes.

—ROWELL'S INN

*C*reate a scarecrow with hay from the farmers market, an old flannel shirt, and blue jeans. Stuff the pants and shirt; tie the body together with a belt or hemp. Add hay-stuffed garden gloves for hands and a hollowed gourd for a head with holes for eyes, nose, and mouth. I built my first scarecrow at Glen-Ella Springs Inn in Clarkesville, Georgia.

Spicebox Venison Roast au Vin Rouge

The spices of autumn are all in this burgundy-and-brandy-roasted venison that you must begin preparing a day ahead of time in order to marinate.

During one trip to a bed-and-breakfast, I visited a gourd farm where kitchen uten-sils are made: funnels, colanders, garlic-keepers, and ladles — all from dried and hol-lowed-out gourds. Sand dry gourds with steel wool or sandpaper and buff them to a shine. Drill holes for a strainer or cut off the gourd's top to make a bowl. From there you can even paint on the outside of the gourd or use it as a Halloween mask.

4	pounds venison roast	1/2	cup olive oil
	Salt and freshly cracked pepper	6	medium carrots, cut into 2-inch pieces
3	bay leaves	12	small white onions, peeled
1/2	teaspoon ground allspice	1/4	cup (1/2 stick) butter
6	whole cloves	1/4	cup all-purpose flour
1/2	cup brandy	10	ounces beef broth
1/2	cup Burgundy wine		

MAKES 8 SERVINGS

*P*lace the venison roast in a large container with a lid. Marinate the meat with salt and pepper, bay leaves, allspice, cloves, brandy, wine, and olive oil. Cover and refrigerate overnight.

The next day transfer the venison with the marinade into a shallow roasting pan. Roast at 350° for 2 to 2 1/2 hours, until the meat is tender. Make sure to baste the venison every 15 to 20 minutes during cooking. About 40 minutes before serving, add the carrots and onions to the baking pan.

Remove the meat and vegetables from the pan. Discard the bay leaves. Measure 1 cup of the pan drippings and combine it with the butter, flour, and beef broth. Simmer over low heat until thickened. Serve this with the venison and roasted vegetables.

—THE BIRCHWOOD INN

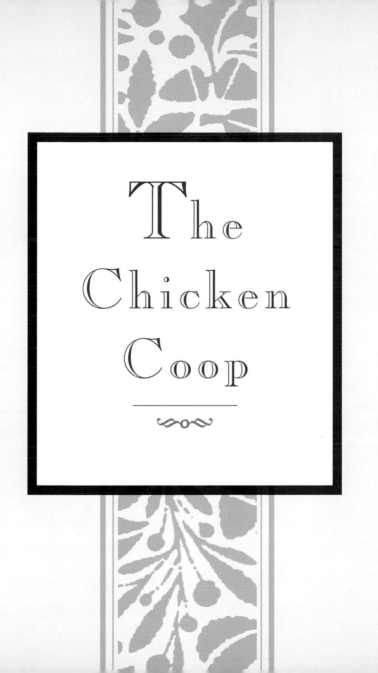

The
Chicken
Coop

Eggs-and-Vegetable Bake

✧

There are egg casseroles and there are egg casseroles. This one is yummy and so versatile that it can even be served as a lazy-day's supper. High Meadows has its own vineyard, with guests helping to harvest the grapes as summer winds down and fall begins.

A cache of seasonal scents permeates the house in fall when you simmer in a kettle of water (on the wood stove or stovetop): 1/4 cup each whole cloves and allspice, 6 or so dried (edible) apples, a few 3-inch cinnamon sticks, and the peels (not the zest) of 1 orange and 1 lemon.

4	slices whole-wheat bread		4	medium tomatoes, coarsely chopped
1/3	cup olive oil		4	eggs
2	large onions, thinly sliced		2	cups milk
1	medium eggplant, cut to a medium dice		1	cup grated Gruyère cheese
2	medium yellow squash, cut to a medium dice		1/3	cup Parmesan cheese
1	green bell pepper, seeded and cut julienne			

MAKES 8 SERVINGS

*A*rrange the bread slices along the bottom of a greased 9x9-inch baking dish. In a large skillet heat the olive oil and sauté the onions and eggplant about 5 minutes. Add the squash and green pepper, continuing to sauté for an additional 10 minutes. Stir in the chopped tomatoes, cover, and simmer for 10 minutes. Pour the vegetable mixture evenly over the bread slices.

Preheat the oven to 350°. In a small bowl, whisk together the eggs and milk until well combined. Stir in the Gruyère cheese and pour the mixture over the bread and vegetables. Sprinkle Parmesan cheese overtop. Bake for 1 hour or until set.

—HIGH MEADOWS INN

Applesauce Egg-and-Bread Pudding

༺∾༄

Innkeeper Joan Wells was encouraged to serve this because it is not too sweet, yet hearty enough for a morning start. The innkeeper was also looking for a casserole that yields less than one egg per serving. For this recipe I prefer the chunky-style applesauce that you can find at farm markets.

16	slices cinnamon or raisin bread		4	teaspoons cinnamon
1/2	cup (1 stick) butter, softened		1/2	teaspoon nutmeg
2	cups unsweetened applesauce		8	eggs
1	cup raisins (optional)		6	cups milk
1	cup lightly packed light brown sugar		1	teaspoon vanilla extract
				Whipped cream for garnish

MAKES 12 SERVINGS

Preheat the oven to 350°. Evenly spread one side of the bread with the butter. Fit half the bread on the bottom of a 3-quart glass baking dish that has been coated with cooking oil spray (or use a nonstick pan). Cut the bread to fit so that the entire bottom is completely covered.

Spread the applesauce on top, followed by the raisins. In a small bowl mix together the brown sugar, cinnamon, and nutmeg. Sprinkle this mixture evenly over the applesauce. Place the remaining bread overtop, butter-side down, filling in all spaces. (The recipe may be refrigerated, covered, overnight at this point.) In a large mixing bowl, whisk the egg, milk, and vanilla. Bake the pudding uncovered for 45 minutes to 1 hour or until lightly puffed and browned. Garnish with whipped cream, if desired.

—THE QUEEN VICTORIA

Pull a little red wagon to the pumpkin patch so you can pick to your heart's content. What a great catch-all for farm shopping!

Wild Mushroom-Stuffed Chicken Breasts with Tarragon Sauce

⌘

Wild mushrooms are more nutritious than button mushrooms and offer meat with a heartier flavor. (You may also use this filling to stuff mushrooms.) The chicken is prepared with a buttery-onion flavor and the sauce is light and tasty. The colors are divine. The White Oak Inn is a traditional country inn where life seems to come into balance.

Chicken and stuffing		Sauce	
1	pound wild mushrooms (such as chanterelles, creminis)	3	tablespoons butter
2	tablespoons butter	1	small onion, finely chopped
1/2	cup finely chopped celery	2	tablespoons all-purpose flour
1	small onion, finely chopped	3/4	cup chicken stock
3/4	cup seasoned breadcrumbs	3/4	cup milk
6	boneless, skinless whole chicken breasts	1/2	teaspoon salt
	Olive oil	1/2	teaspoon pepper
	Paprika	2	teaspoons finely chopped fresh tarragon
		1/2	cup dry white wine
		1/2	cup half-and-half

MAKES 6 SERVINGS

*P*reheat the oven to 350°. Begin the stuffing by finely chopping half of the mushrooms. Cut the remaining mushrooms into thin slices and set aside. Melt the butter in a skillet. Add the chopped mushrooms, celery, and onions. Sauté the mixture over high heat for about 5 minutes, or until the onions are translucent. Stir in the breadcrumbs and continue to cook a few minutes to incorporate. Remove from the heat; set aside.

Open the chicken breasts and arrange them on a flat surface. Evenly divide the stuffing mixture among the breasts, spreading to within 1/2 inch of the edge. Fold over and seal. Brush the chicken with a coating of olive oil and sprinkle with paprika. Bake 40 minutes.

Meanwhile, Prepare the sauce. Melt the butter in a small saucepan. Add the reserved mushroom slices and chopped onion and sauté for about 5 minutes. Stir in the flour and continue to cook. When the flour is incorporated, whisk in the chicken stock and milk. Add the salt, pepper, and tarragon. Simmer gently about 3 minutes, or until the seasonings have blended. Whisk in the wine and simmer another 3 minutes. Blend in the half-and-half. Serve warm over the chicken breasts.

— THE WHITE OAK INN

Lemon-and-Rosemary Roasted Chicken with Apples and Mushrooms

‿o‿

After baking the chicken in a bath of maple syrup, lemon juice, and rosemary, a sauté of mushrooms and apples is prepared with an herbed quinoa. Quinoa (keen-wah), a beadlike grain just becoming familiar to Americans, is available at farm markets that also carry whole grains and edible seeds. The mother grain of the ancient Incas, it is lighter than rice and is considered a complete protein because it contains all eight essential amino acids. Tasting like couscous, quinoa may be substituted for wild rice in this recipe.

Chicken

1	2-pound chicken, cut in half, wings removed and saved for another recipe
1/4	cup pure maple syrup
	Juice from 1 lemon
1	sprig rosemary

Mushrooms

1/2	ounce olive oil
2	small leeks (white part), cleaned and sliced
1/4	pound shiitake mushrooms, thinly sliced
1/4	pound oyster mushrooms, thinly sliced

3	McIntosh apples, peeled and thinly sliced

Herbed quinoa

1/2	pound quinoa or wild rice
2	cups chicken stock
1/2	bunch fresh tarragon, chopped (or 1/2 tablespoon dried)
1/2	bunch fresh thyme, chopped (or 1/2 tablespoon dried)
1/2	bunch fresh basil, chopped (or 1/2 tablespoon dried)
	Salt and pepper

MAKES 4 SERVINGS

*P*reheat the oven to 350°. Place the chicken in a roasting dish with the maple syrup, lemon juice, and rosemary. Roast for 20 minutes. Reduce the temperature to 225° and bake for another 15 minutes or longer until browned basting occasionally.

Meanwhile, heat the olive oil in a large skillet. When the oil is hot, sauté the leeks until tender. Add the shiitake and oyster mushrooms and apples and continue to cook for about 5 minutes. Keep warm while preparing the rice.

In a large saucepan cook the quinoa and chicken stock, covered, over low heat for about 20 minutes or until the rice absorbs the stock. Fold in the tarragon, thyme, and basil, and season with salt and pepper.

To serve, slice the chicken leg and thigh away from the breast and arrange over the herbed rice. Pour the mushroom-apple sauté among the chicken pieces. Drizzle the entire plate with pan drippings.

—STONE MANOR

The Pie Safe

PICTURE FACING CHAPTER OPENER: THE DINING ROOM AT CRANE HOUSE B&B FEATURES A WONDERFUL OLD PIE SAFE, COUNTLESS OTHER ANTIQUES, AND A WHOLE COLLECTION OF TASTY PIES PREPARED BY LUE CRANE.

Apple Cider Doughnuts with Maple Glaze

The editors of *Eating Well* magazine cleverly used a mini-bundt pan to make these doughnuts. These treats are great fun for pre-game parties or tailgate dinners. Certainly, they will get a nod of approval at fall tea-time gatherings. These are also nice with 3/4 of a cup of coarsely chopped walnuts added to the batter.

Doughnuts

3	tablespoons white sugar
2	cups all-purpose flour
1½	teaspoons baking powder
1½	teaspoons baking soda
½	teaspoon salt
2	teaspoons cinnamon
1	egg, lightly beaten
⅔	cup firmly packed brown sugar
½	cup sweetened or unsweetened apple butter
⅓	cup pure maple syrup
⅓	cup fresh apple cider
⅓	cup nonfat plain yogurt
3	tablespoons canola oil

Glaze

1¼	cups powdered sugar, sifted
1	teaspoon vanilla extract
½ to ⅓	cup pure maple syrup

Apple cider is reason enough to visit the farmers market. Sample a cup while shopping. Take a quart home and mix it with a quart of cranberry juice, 2 tablespoons brown sugar, two small cinnamon sticks, 8 whole cloves, a sprinkling of pumpkin pie spice. Bring the mixture to a boil. Simmer, covered, for 10 minutes, and serve.

*P*reheat the oven to 400°. Prepare the pan. Coat a nonstick mini-bundt pan with vegetable spray. Sprinkle with half of the white sugar, shaking out the excess.

In a medium mixing bowl whisk together the flour, baking powder, baking soda, salt, and cinnamon. Set aside. In a larger bowl, whisk together the egg, brown sugar, apple butter, maple syrup, cider, yogurt, and oil. Add the dry ingredients, stirring just until moistened. Divide half the batter among the prepared molds, spooning 2 generous tablespoonfuls of batter per mold.

Bake 10 to 12 minutes or until the tops spring back when touched lightly. Loosen the edges of the cakes and turn out onto a rack to cool. Clean the bundt pan, then recoat with cooking oil/spray and sugar. Fill the molds with the remaining batter. Bake again and repeat the process.

Meanwhile, prepare the glaze. In a medium bowl, combine the powdered sugar and vanilla. Gradually whisk in enough maple syrup to make a coating consistency.

Dip the shaped (underside) side of the doughnuts in the glaze to coat the tops. Let the glaze drip down the sides. Set the cakes glaze-side up on a rack over waxed paper for a few minutes until the glaze has set. Serve.

—GAIL'S KITCHEN

Upside-Down Pear-and-Cranberry Cake

The seasonal aspect of this dessert is enhanced by the way it is cooked and served. The recipe calls for using a nonstick pan, but you may also use a greased iron skillet and serve it right out of the pan with a dollop of vanilla ice cream.

WINDFLOWER INN, GREAT BARRINGTON, MASSACHUSETTS

The Inn at Maplewood Farm has developed a way to save autumn's apple crop for tea, baked goods, or in oatmeal—make apple honey. Process six tart, peeled, and seeded apples, and add to a pot with three cups sugar; one tablespoon honey; zest of one orange; and one-half cup apple juice. Bring to a boil, and simmer for forty minutes. Add two tablespoons of apple liqueur, cooking five minutes more. Makes four (eight-ounce) jars. Store in refrigerator up to thirty days.

3	medium sweet ripe pears, peeled, cored, and thinly sliced	$^1/_2$	cup white sugar
		3	eggs, room temperature
1	teaspoon cinnamon	2	teaspoons vanilla extract
$^1/_4$	teaspoon nutmeg	2	tablespoons cranberry liqueur
$1^1/_2$	cups all-purpose flour	$^2/_3$	cup lightly packed brown sugar
$1^1/_2$	teaspoons baking powder		
$^3/_4$	cup ($1^1/_2$ sticks), plus 3 tablespoons unsalted butter, softened	$^1/_3$	cup whole cranberries, fresh, frozen, or dried

MAKES 4 TO 6 SERVINGS

*P*lace *pear slices in a glass pie plate. Sprinkle the pears lightly with cinnamon and nutmeg and place in the microwave on medium–high for 2 minutes to soften.*

Preheat the oven to 375°. In a small bowl mix together the flour and baking powder. In a large mixing bowl beat the $1^1/_2$ sticks of butter until pale and creamy. Add the white sugar and beat until light and fluffy. Add the eggs, one at a time, beating after each one. Mix in the vanilla. Fold the flour mixture into the batter just until no white streaks remain. Do not overmix. Stir in the cranberry liqueur. Set the batter aside.

In a 9-inch, oven-proof, nonstick skillet, melt the remaining 3 tablespoons of butter. Add the brown sugar and cook over moderate heat until melted and bubbly. Remove the skillet from the heat and toss the cranberries in the pan. Arrange the pear slices in circles over the mixture. Begin with the outer circle and work in. Spread the batter evenly over the pear slices.

Bake in the oven approximately 25 minutes or until tester comes clean. Allow the cake to cool for 5 minutes and then invert it onto a large platter. Serve warm.

—THE WINDFLOWER INN

Pumpkin Bread Pudding with Caramel Sauce

∽०∼

I love bread puddings and have one best suited to every season. The Inn at Cedar Falls' recipe has now become my choice for fall. Feel free to experiment with other sweet quick breads instead of the pumpkin called for here.

Vidalia onions have hardly any calories and are sweet when baked. Here is a quick recipe from Fearrington House: Cut the top from the Vidalia and season with salt and pepper, chives, parsley, thyme. Top with 1/2 tablespoon butter and wrap in aluminum foil. Bake at 375° for 35 minutes or until tender.

Pudding

5	large eggs
1/2	cup sugar
2	cups half-and-half
1 1/2	cups evaporated skim milk
1	tablespoon vanilla extract
1	loaf pumpkin bread, cut into 1/2-inch cubes
3/4	cup golden raisins

Caramel Sauce

1/2	cup (1 stick) butter, cut into pieces
1/2	cup firmly packed light brown sugar
1/2	cup white granulated sugar
1/2	cup milk
1	teaspoon vanilla extract

MAKES 6 TO 8 SERVINGS

*P*reheat the oven to 325°. Grease a 9x13-inch baking pan or 6 or 8 (3-inch) custard cups. In a medium bowl, beat the eggs until frothy. Mix in the sugar. When combined, gradually stir in the half-and-half, evaporated milk, and vanilla.

Arrange the bread cubes and raisins in the prepared baking pan. Pour the milk mixture overtop and gently combine. Bake the pudding for 50 to 60 minutes or until a tester comes clean.

Meanwhile, prepare the caramel sauce. Combine the butter, sugars, and milk in a heavy saucepan. Stir over low heat until the sugars dissolve and the butter melts. Increase the heat and boil for 1 minute. Stir in the vanilla and serve warm over the pumpkin bread pudding.

—THE INN AT CEDAR FALLS

Steamed Persimmon Pudding with Lemon-Orange Sauce

∽○∽

I went persimmon picking at San Ysidro Ranch, a country inn in Santa Barbara, California. Persimmons grow on a tree there and, as in other parts of the country, are picked in October. They are a good source of vitamins A and C, but it is essential to eat them only when ripe, or they will pucker your taste buds with incredible astringency. Choose fruits at the farmers market that are plump and soft or ripen them at room temperature.

FALL JOURNEYS TO THE FARMERS MARKET LEAD TO ROMANTIC WALKS DOWN LEAF-LINED FOREST PATHS

Pudding

1	cup puréed persimmons (strained through a colander to remove seeds and skins)
2	teaspoons baking soda
1/2	cup (1 stick) margarine
1 1/2	cups sugar
2	eggs
1	tablespoon lemon juice
2	tablespoons rum
1	cup all-purpose flour
1	teaspoon cinnamon
1/2	teaspoon salt
1	cup chopped walnuts or pecans
1	cup raisins

Sauce

1	tablespoon cornstarch
1/4	cup sugar
1	cup orange juice
1 1/2	tablespoons lemon juice
1	teaspoon grated lemon zest

MAKES 8 SERVINGS

*F*ill a pot that is large enough to hold a 2-quart pudding mold with enough water to come halfway up the sides of the mold. Place a rack or mason jar ring in the bottom of the pot, allowing the water to circulate freely while steaming. Set the pot over medium heat and bring the water to a boil.

Meanwhile, in a small bowl combine the persimmon purée and the baking soda. Set aside, allowing the mixture to stiffen a bit. In a separate bowl cream the margarine and sugar until smooth. Add the eggs, lemon juice, and rum. Beat well. Stir in the flour, cinnamon, and salt. When the batter is thoroughly blended, add the persimmon mixture and beat well. Stir in the nuts and raisins.

Generously coat the 2-quart mold with cooking oil spray. Spoon in the pudding mixture and set the mold on the rack in the pot of boiling water. Cover tightly and steam over medium heat for 2 hours. Remove the mold from the pot and let it rest for 5 minutes. Gently turn the pudding onto a rack, cooling slightly before serving.

Prepare the lemon sauce. In a small saucepan combine the cornstarch and sugar. Slowly whisk in the orange juice. Stirring constantly, cook the mixture over low heat until it thickens and comes to a boil. Stir in the lemon juice and zest. Serve warm over the persimmon pudding.

—THE MANOR AT TAYLOR'S STORE

Apple Butter Pumpkin Pie
with Streusel Topping

◦◦◦

Author and TV chef Marcia Adams was a guest one day on the set of my TV show at the Checkerberry Inn in Goshen, Indiana. Marcia gave me an autographed copy of her book *Heirloom Recipes*. This incredible pumpkin pie is only one of the examples of traditional recipes in the book that have Marcia's down-home delicious interpretations. Imagine apple butter added to a pumpkin pie!

This has become the pumpkin pie I make in my kitchen. Thanks Marcia. With this recipe I know I will, as she says on *her* show, "Eat good."

Filling

3	large eggs
1	cup pumpkin purée
1	cup sweetened or unsweetened apple butter
1/2	cup firmly packed dark brown sugar
2	teaspoons angostura bitters
1/2	teaspoon cinnamon
1/2	teaspoon ground ginger
1/2	teaspoon nutmeg
1/4	teaspoon salt

1	cup evaporated milk

Pie

Pastry for a deep 9-inch pie shell

Streusel Topping

1/2	cup all-purpose flour
1/3	cup firmly packed dark brown sugar
1/3	cup coarsely chopped pecans
3	tablespoons butter, softened

MAKES 8 TO 10 SERVINGS

*P*reheat the oven to 375°. In a medium bowl beat the eggs slightly with a hand beater, then blend in the pumpkin purée, apple butter, sugar, bitters, spices, and salt until the spices are thoroughly incorporated. Add the milk and beat until well combined.

Line a 9-inch deep-dish pie plate with the pastry shell. Pour the filling into the unbaked shell and bake the pie for 50 to 60 minutes or until a tester inserted comes clean.

Meanwhile, prepare the streusel topping. In a small bowl combine the flour, brown sugar, and pecans. Whisk in the butter. Sprinkle the streusel over the top of the pie and bake for an additional 15 minutes. Cool slightly, then serve warm with a dollop of whipped cream or a scoop of ice cream, if desired.

—GAIL'S KITCHEN

Cranberry Walnut Tart
with Buttery Fall Leaves

〜o〜

Make the dough ahead of time. This recipe has a few steps but is well worth the time.

Pastry

10	tablespoons chilled unsalted butter, divided
3	tablespoons sugar
$1/4$	teaspoon salt
7	tablespoons ice water
$1^3/4$	cups all-purpose flour

Filling

1	egg
$1/8$	teaspoon salt
1	cup toasted walnuts, coarsely chopped
2	pears, peeled, cored, quartered
1	cup sugar
$2/3$	cup pure maple syrup
4	cups cranberries
$1/4$	cup ($1/2$ stick) unsalted butter
$4^1/2$	teaspoons bourbon

In a food processor, pulse butter, sugar, and salt a few seconds. Add the water and blend until coarse crumbs form. Add the flour and process to form dough. Do not make a ball. Cover the dough in plastic wrap and refrigerate until firm, at least 2 hours.

Roll the dough on a floured surface to a 1/8-inch-thick round. Transfer to an ungreased 11-inch tart or pie pan with a removable bottom. Press the dough into the pan. Trim off excess dough (setting it aside in the refrigerator), leaving a 1/4-inch overhang. Crimp to form a decorative edge. Refrigerate for 15 minutes, uncovered. Preheat the oven to 425°. Line the tart pastry with aluminum foil and fill it with pie weights. Bake 15 minutes to set. Remove the foil and weights. Pierce the pastry with a fork and bake until lightly browned, about 10 minutes. Turn the oven to 375°.

While the tart shell bakes, prepare the filling. In a clean bowl of the processor blend the egg with the salt. Set it aside as a glaze for the maple-leaf garnish.

Sprinkle the walnuts over the crust. In a clean processor bowl, blend the pears and sugar. While the machine runs, pour in the maple syrup. Transfer the pear mixture to a 10-inch nonstick skillet. Bring the mixture to a boil over high heat and cook for 5 minutes, stirring frequently. Add the cranberries and cook until they have popped, about 8 minutes.

Transfer the mixture to the food processor with the butter, bourbon, and salt. Coarsely chop the cranberries, pulsing about 2 times (do not purée). Cool to room temperature.

Spoon the filling into the crust, smoothing with a rubber spatula. Roll reserved dough scraps onto a floured surface to 1/8-inch thickness. Cut 8 leaf decorations, using as a pattern a 2 1/2 inch-wide maple leaf or a cardboard template. Brush the tops of the leaves with the reserved egg glaze. Arrange the leaves around the outer edge of the pie. The filling will still show through the center. Set on a baking sheet. Bake the pie for about 35 minutes or until the leaves are golden. Cool completely.

—BLACK RIVER INN

Lattice Squash Pie with Lemon and Cinnamon

With their patchwork quilt design, lattice pies are always a picturesque addition to the fall table. This recipe has been in innkeeper Marguerite Swanson's recipe box since she was a young girl. It is tried and true!

Filling

1	tablespoon instant tapioca
3	cups sliced, cooked yellow squash
1¼	cups sugar
1	egg, slightly beaten
¼	teaspoon salt
2	teaspoons lemon extract
½	teaspoon vanilla extract

Pastry

2	cups all-purpose flour
½	teaspoon salt
⅔	cup shortening
⅓ to ½	cup cold water

Assembly

1	tablespoon butter
1	teaspoon cinnamon
2	tablespoons sugar

MAKES 8 SERVINGS

*P*reheat the oven to 450°. In a large mixing bowl stir the tapioca into the squash. Beat at low speed with an electric mixer. Add sugar, egg, salt, and lemon and vanilla extracts. Beat again until smooth and incorporated.

In a medium bowl, stir together the flour and salt. Cut in the shortening until the mixture forms coarse crumbs. Sprinkle 1 tablespoon of cold water over an isolated part of the mixture. Toss with a fork and push to the side of the bowl. Repeat until all of the mixture is moistened. Gather the dough into a ball and divide in half.

On a lightly floured surface flatten one of the balls with your hands. Roll the dough from the center to the edge, forming a 12-inch circle. Ease the dough into an ungreased 9-inch pie plate, being careful to avoid stretching the pastry. Trim the dough to ½ inch beyond the edge of the pie plate.

For the top crust, roll out the second ball of dough. Cut the dough into ½- to ¾-inch wide strips using a pastry wheel or knife.

To assemble, pour the squash filling into the unbaked pie shell. Dot with the 1 tablespoon of butter. Cover with the lattice pastry, alternating the strips, under and over each piece. Combine the cinnamon and sugar, sprinkle overtop, and bake 15 minutes. Reduce the oven to 350° and bake 45 minutes longer or until the crust is golden.

—DURHAM HOUSE

[107]

*H*azelnut Pumpkin Cheesecake Roll *with Brandied Chocolate Sauce*

వొం

Whenever I serve this easy but elegant jellyroll cake, it never fails to get rave reviews. While particularly complementary for fall, it is refreshing to serve any time of the year and always makes a splendid presentation. The chocolate sauce is optional, as the cake is moist and rich without the sauce. But be indulgent once in awhile!

Cake

3	eggs
1	cup sugar
2/3	cup puréed pumpkin
1	teaspoon lemon juice
3/4	cup all-purpose flour
2	teaspoons cinnamon
1	teaspoon baking powder
1	teaspoon ground ginger
1/2	teaspoon salt
1/2	teaspoon nutmeg
1	cup finely chopped hazelnuts

Filling

1	cup powdered sugar
2	3-ounce packages cream cheese
1	teaspoon maple extract

Sauce

3/4	cup water
1/3	cup honey
2	ounces unsweetened chocolate
1	teaspoon vanilla extract
1	teaspoon brandy, optional

Assembly

	Mint for garnish

*P*reheat the oven to 375°. In a large mixing bowl beat the eggs with an electric mixer on high speed for 5 minutes or until thick and pale yellow in color. Gradually beat in the sugar. Stir in the pumpkin and the lemon juice.

In a separate small bowl combine the flour, cinnamon, baking powder, ginger, salt, and nutmeg. Fold into the egg-and-pumpkin mixture. Grease and flour a 15x10x1-inch baking pan. Pour the batter evenly into the pan. Sprinkle the hazelnuts evenly overtop the batter.

Bake in the oven for 15 minutes or until a tester comes clean. Meanwhile, place a kitchen towel on a flat surface and sprinkle it evenly with a thin layer of powdered sugar. Remove the cake from the oven and invert onto the towel. Roll up the cake with the towel, jellyroll style, starting from the short end of the cake. Allow to cool completely in the towel, about 30 minutes.

Meanwhile, prepare the filling. In a small mixing bowl beat the 1 cup of powdered sugar, cream cheese, margarine, and maple extract with an electric mixer on medium speed until smooth. Unroll the cooled cake. Spread the filling evenly over the cake and re-roll. Cover the cake and chill it for about 1 hour.

When ready to serve, prepare the sauce. In a small saucepan over medium-high heat stir the water and honey together until incorporated. Add the chocolate and stir until melted. Add the vanilla and brandy and stir until incorporated.

To serve, cut the cake into 1-inch slices and place on dessert plates. Drape a few tablespoons of the warm chocolate sauce on top of the cake and add a sprig of mint for garnish.

—GAIL'S KITCHEN

*W*hite Oak Inn makes a ginger butter to serve with 2 cups each of squash, green beans, and corn. Combine 1 tablespoon butter, melted with 1 tablespoon chopped ginger root, 2 tablespoons lemon juice, and a twist of black peppercorns.

Apple Orchard Dumplings with Cinnamon Syrup

∽◦∾

There is something about an apple dumpling that generously implies homey comfort food. This dessert is easy to prepare and nice served after dinner. Let it accompany either a fancy meal in the dining room or serve it by a campfire with everyone wrapped in wool blankets.

Syrup

1/3	cup all-purpose flour
1 1/2	cups sugar
1/4	teaspoon cinnamon
1/4	teaspoon salt
1 1/2	cups water
1 1/2	tablespoons margarine

Pastry

2	cups all-purpose flour
1/2	teaspoon salt
3/4	cup vegetable shortening
1/2	cup cold water

Assembly

6	medium Ida Red apples, peeled, and cored
1	teaspoon cinnamon
1	cup sugar

MAKES 6 DUMPLINGS

In a small saucepan, combine the flour, sugar, cinnamon, salt, and water. Bring to a boil over medium heat, stirring continuously. Add the margarine and stir until incorporated. Remove the saucepan from the heat and let it cool at room temperature.

Preheat the oven to 375°. Prepare the pastry. In a large bowl mix together the flour and salt and cut in the shortening with a pastry blender or 2 knives until the mixture forms coarse crumbs. Add the cold water and stir until the flour is just moistened. On a lightly floured surface roll the dough into a rectangle of about 12x18 inches. Divide the dough into 6 6-inch squares. Place a whole peeled and cored apple onto each square. Mix the sugar and cinnamon together and sprinkle each apple with the mixture. Fold the dough around each apple bringing the four corners up to the center; pinch the dough to seal tightly.

Place the dumplings on an ungreased large jellyroll pan or an 11 1/2 x 7 1/2 x 1 1/2 inch pan, or bake in (4 to 6- inch) individual baking dishes. Bake for 40 minutes or until the dumplings are soft and the pastry is golden brown.

—CRANE HOUSE B&B

Layered Apple-and-Nut Cream Cheese Pastry

~o~

Crane House B&B is situated by a bucolic u-pick farm. Apple orchards supply the entire Crane family with fresh ingredients for their cider mill and Pie Pantry restaurant. This recipe is called a strudel on the menu, but the Cranes agree that it is something between a strudel and a pie, at least in form. It is so popular that the Cranes keep on making this whatever-you-wanna-call-it, and you will, too.

Apple filling

3	cups (4 Ida Red apples), peeled, cored, and thinly sliced
1/2	cup water
3/4	cup sugar
1/3	cup all-purpose flour
1/4	teaspoon salt
1/2	teaspoon cinnamon

Cheese filling

8	ounces cream cheese
1/3	cup sugar
1	egg
1/3	cup lukewarm water

Crust

1 1/2	cups all-purpose flour
1/3	cup sugar
1/4	teaspoon salt
1 1/4	cups shortening
1/2	cup margarine
1/2	cup cold water

Assembly

3/4	cup coarsely chopped walnuts
	Pastry apple for garnish, optional

Farmers markets offer the best in fresh produce, as well as overripe fruits and vegetables for a great price. The latter have terrific flavors for cooking. I spend autumn putting up fruits and soups to cook for my inn guests in winter.
—Claudia Ryan, Windflower Inn

Prepare the filling first. In a large saucepan simmer the apple slices in the water for about 5 minutes. Add the sugar, flour, salt, and cinnamon. Stir the mixture and put it aside to cool.

In a medium mixing bowl mix together the cream cheese, sugar, and egg with an electric mixer at medium speed. Gradually add the lukewarm water and mix until incorporated. Set aside.

In a separate bowl prepare the crust. Combine the flour, sugar, and salt with the shortening and the margarine. Cut the mixture with a pastry blender or 2 knives until it forms coarse crumbs. Add the cold water and stir until the flour is well moistened. The dough may be sticky.

On a floured board, roll out a portion of the dough into a 13-inch (⅛-inch-thick) round. Place the dough into a 9-inch round cake pan, letting the dough hang over the sides of the pan. Spread half of the cream cheese mixture over the pastry.

Roll 2 (6-inch circles), ⅛-inch thick, out of the dough. Place 1 circle on top of the cream cheese. Add the apple filling on top of the circle and then add the chopped nuts. Top with the remaining cream cheese. Fold the excess pastry overtop the cream cheese. There should be enough to completely seal the top, but if it is slightly open that is okay. You may save a little excess dough and make a cutout in the shape of an apple with stem and seal it to the top of the crust with a little water.

Bake for 40 minutes or until golden brown. Sprinkle with sugar. Cool and serve by cutting pie-like wedges.

—CRANE HOUSE B&B

Directory

Bear Creek Lodge
1184 Bear Creek Tr.
Victor, MT 59875
(406) 642-3750

Rooms: 8

Surrounded by pine trees, this rustic mountain hideaway is constructed of logs harvested near Yellowstone Park. Mountain meadows, ponds, creeks, and the Selway–Bitteroot Wilderness are just a short hike from the lodge.

Benbow Inn
445 Lake Benbow Dr.
Garberville, CA 95542
(707) 923-2124

Rooms: 55

A baronial-style Tudor mansion, towering and impressive as the redwoods nearby, Benbow has been an inn since 1926 and serving afternoon tea and scones is still popular here.

Birchwood Inn
Route 45
Temple, NH 03084
(603) 878-3285

Rooms: 7

Guest rooms at this New Hampshire inn farmhouse are adorned with antiques and homemade quilts. The small, candlelit dining room features Rufus Porter murals.

Black River Inn
100 Main St.
Ludlow, VT 05149
(802) 228-5585

Rooms: 10

Antique bed chambers with feather pillows and etched lighting fixtures beckon you to another life with all of the comforts of the modern world, too.

PICTURE FACING DIRECTORY OPENER: A RESPITE ON THE PORCH ON A COOL AUTUMN DAY AT CRANE HOUSE B&B

Blueberry Hill
R.D. 3
Goshen, VT 05733
(802) 247-6735

Rooms: 12

Situated amidst Vermont's Green
Mountain National Forest, this tranquil
inn offers scenic year-round sports activi-
ties. Cross-country skiing, biking, and hik-
ing are just steps away.

The Captain Freeman Inn
15 Breakwater Rd.
Brewster, Cape Cod, MA 02631
(508) 896-7481

Rooms: 12

Built in 1866, this Victorian-era sea
captain's mansion is just a short stroll from
the beaches of Cape Cod Bay. Spring and
summer bring breakfast poolside on the
screened-in wraparound porch; during
winter, breakfast is by fireside in the cozy
dining room.

The Crane House
6051 124th Ave. (M-89)
Fennville, MI 49408
(616) 561-6931

Rooms: 5

Primitive former pioneer home with
feather beds, handmade quilts, and a 1900
parlor stove. The Cranes also host the Pie
Pantry Restaurant across the street where
they serve old-fashioned lunches, dinners
and hundreds of fruit pies in a nostalgic
setting. You can watch the cider being
pressed in the fall or pick apples in the
orchard.

Durham House
921 Heights Blvd.
Houston, TX 77008
(713) 868-4654

Rooms: 5

This Queen Anne Victorian, on the
National Register of Historic Places, features a garden gazebo and original mystery
weekends.

The Fearrington House
2000 Fearrington Village Center
Pittsboro, NC 27312
(919) 542-2121

Rooms: 15

Beautiful gardens and rolling country-
side encircle this classic inn. It is built
around a center courtyard, and each guest
room exudes its own distinctive character.
The four-star restaurant features sophisti-
cated regional cuisine.

The Governor's Inn
86 Main St.
Ludlow, VT 05149
(802) 228-8830

Rooms: 7

This romantic Victorian inn is known
for its attention to detail, fine craftsman-
ship, and numerous culinary awards.

High Meadows Inn
Route 4, Box 6
Scottsville, VA 24590
(804) 286-2218

Rooms: 12

Virginia's vineyard inn is situated in
the heart of the state's breathtaking wine
country. The nineteenth-century
European-style house offers elegant candlelight dining and enchanting guest rooms.

The Inn at Blackberry Farm
1471 West Millers Cover Rd.
Walland, TN 37886
(404) 971-6475

Rooms: 23

The mist in the valley complements the
romance of this distinguished inn that dis-
plays the innkeepers' passion for flowers
and impeccable decorating taste.

The Inn at Cedar Falls
21190 St. Rt. 374
Logan, OH 43138
(614) 385-7489

Rooms: 9 rooms, 6 cabins

This rustic log cabin inn is surrounded by the natural beauty of the Appalachian foothills. Mountain-style folk furniture and rag rugs create a cozy and authentic environment.

The Inn at Maplewood Farm
447 Center Road
Hillsborough, NH. 03244
(603) 464-4242

Rooms: 4

Quiet country farmhouse where guests sip lemonade on a wicker-filled front porch, overlooking a meadow of black-and-white cows.

The Inn at Olde New Berlin
321 Market St.
New Berlin, PA 17855-0390
(717) 966-0321

Rooms: 5

A turn-of-the-century turreted Victorian, this in-town country retreat combines gracious hospitality and inviting decor.

The Lakehouse on Golden Pond
Shelley Hill Rd.
Stanfordville, NY 12581
(914) 266-8093

Rooms: 7

Imagine a lakefront view on a pond in the Hudson River Valley. No wonder the painters of the Hudson River Valley School were so inspired. Walk to the pond and sit on the dock or stay inside and be cozy by the fire.

Ledford Mill and Museum
Route 2, Box 152
Wartrace, TN 37183
(615) 455-2546

Rooms: 1

Privacy is guaranteed in this one-suite, nineteenth-century grist mill, hidden in the serene Tennessee wilderness.

The Manor at Taylor's Store
Route 1, Box 533
Wirtz, VA 24184
(540) 721-3951

Rooms: 6

Enter this eighteenth-century estate through massive brick columns and pass the original granary from Taylor's Store. The beautifully restored plantation home offers guests gracious southern hospitality, fine cuisine, five ponds, and an old log house filled with the innkeepers' quilts.

Maplewood Inn
Route 22A S
Fair Haven, VT 05743
(802) 265-8039

Rooms: 5

This Greek Revival inn from 1843 contains a unique tavern furnished with various period styles and antiques.

The Queen Victoria
102 Ocean St.
Cape May, NJ 08204
(609) 884-8702

Rooms: 23

This restored grand Victorian mansion in the heart of Cape May's historic district is picturesque, stately, and most inviting.

Ravenscroft Inn
533 Quincy St.
Port Townsend, WA 98368
(360) 385-2784

Rooms: 9

Resting high on a bluff overlooking the
city of Port Townsend and the entrance to
Puget Sound, Ravenscroft's well-appoint-
ed guest rooms feature spectacular views
and simple comforts.

Rowell's Inn
R.R. #1, Box 267-D
Simonsville, VT 05143
(802) 875-3658

Rooms: 5

Once a stagecoach stop, post office, and
general store, this versatile New England
building became an inn in 1900 when F.
A. Rowell purchased the property. Sleep
where the town's VIPs once danced the
night away.

Seven Sisters Inn
820 Southeast Fort King St.
Ocala, FL 34471
(904) 867-1170

Rooms: 7

The airline pilot innkeepers are full of
life and reflect that in the decor and food.
This is an outstanding Florida inn.

Stone Manor
5820 Carroll Boycr Rd.
Middletown, MD 21769
(301) 473-5454

Rooms: 5

An eighteenth-century farmhouse set on
114 acres of fertile farmland, the manor
has a restaurant renowned for its use of
local produce, home-baked breads, and
well-stocked wine cellar.

The White Oak Inn
29683 Walhonding (S.R. 715)
Danville, OH 43014
(614) 599-6107

Rooms: 10

Country pleasures abound in this
secluded Ohio farmhouse. Guests can par-
ticipate in on-site archeological digs or
relax on the inn's front porch swings.

Windflower Inn
684 South Egremont Rd.
Great Barrington, MA 01230
(413) 528-2720

Rooms: 13

Built in 1820, this Federal-style inn is
spacious and peaceful with plenty of fire-
places. The dining room features whimsical
Currier & Ives scenes as well as paintings
by local New England artists.

Windham Hill Inn
R.R. 1, Box 44
West Townshend, VT 05359
(802) 874-4080

Rooms: 18

Windham Hill sits at the end of a
wooded country road, hidden from the
pressures of reality. So much here, inside
and out, can revitalize the weary traveler.

Index